MW01537573

The Gospel According to a Black Woman

Ebony Adedayo

AYA
Media and Publishing

Adedayo, Ebony J.
The Gospel According to a Black Woman
Includes bibliographical references
1. Women, Black 2. African American women 3. Spirituality
4. Race 5. Poetry
ISBN: 9798678020376

© 2020 by Ebony Adedayo, Aya Media and Publishing, LLC
All rights reserved.
Reprint or reproduction, even partially, in all forms is strictly prohibited
without express written permission from the author.

Dedicated to my grandmother, Elee Brown.

May you rest in peace.

Table of Contents

Adedayo

Introduction

I must be honest. When I initially landed on the title of this book, The Gospel According to a Black Woman, *I hesitated. I wondered if by calling it "The Gospel" I was doing too much. Was I being too boastful or even bordering on sacrilege and blasphemy?*

But the meaning of the word derives from the Koine Greek word *euaggelion* (transliterated), which means *good news* or *truth.* Historically, this word has mostly been used in Christian circles, specifically by disciples of Jesus to testify about his works of healing, deliverance, and salvation. The first four books of the New Testament—Matthew, Mark, Luke, and John—claim this, opening their respective works with the phrase "The Gospel According to . . ." to assert spiritual authority. This assertion was necessary in the face of extreme violence from the Roman Empire, who silenced anyone posing a threat to their kingdom. Claiming spiritual authority outside of Rome was not only a radical act; it was also a deadly one.

As I ruminated on this title, I questioned whether I could apply the same literary device as these authors did. In stating and naming my truth, my witness, could I be so bold as to take the word and claim it as my own? As you can see, I landed on yes. I said yes because the truth of my experience navigating systems—the government, the church, the academy, the nonprofit sector, the business sector—is valid. My perspective as a Black woman in the United States in 2020 is valid. My witness is truth, regardless of the credentials I hold or whether anyone else will believe or validate me. And for me to speak this truth AND claim spiritual authority is critical in our society that continuously ignores and devalues Black women.

In the original title, I qualified Black Woman with the word "liberated." There were reasons for this. When I first compiled this collection of poems and reflections back in 2017, I initially thought of them as a story, showing how I confronted some areas of my life to find healing and liberation. As I continued to write and revise my original manuscript, I saw that this book collection was bigger than the truth of my journey. Although it includes the story of my journey, it is also about the truth of so many other Black women with whom I share similar stories of triumph, struggle, heartache, and pain.

I also removed the word "liberated" because I did not want to use it as a barometer to validate my witness. For the same reason, I am careful not to list or boast about other qualifiers here—not because they don't exist, but because the world needs to become more comfortable listening to Black women. Period. We need not prove our worth through our education, expertise, social media following, occupation, marital status, religion, ministerial credentials, or any other thing that exists (though we often possess all these qualifiers and are still not taken seriously). We can and will exist as we are!

Before I close out this introduction, I must also state that this is not a Christian book, though I am a Christian. I affirm, along with the late James Cone that Jesus is the truth of my story. Yet and still, Jesus is not my only story. I also carry the story of someone whose ancestors were enslaved. I carry the story of estrangement, isolation, and depression in my family of origin. I carry the story of a people, who despite what they faced, resisted and carved out pathways for them to exist. I carry the story of women who have faced seemingly insurmountable obstacles in the boardroom, the classroom, the pulpit, and in the streets, regardless of what we were wearing. These stories come together in compounding and sometimes contradictory ways to create a new meta-narrative that helps me make sense of who I am, where I am going, and how I see the world.

Recently, I have been absolutely in love with a song by Jamila Woods called "Holy." Borrowing from Psalms 23 and the Lord's Prayer, which is found in Matthew 6 and Luke 11 of the Bible, the lyrics explicitly state and name the holiness bound up in Black women's bodies. As they are. We already are. What a radical notion! It is radical because it is a notion outside of many theological frameworks that stress original sin or inherent unrighteousness, particularly regarding Black women. In the United States, the Black body is the definition of sin. But Black women, because we live at the intersection of race and gender-based violence (and more if we are differently abled, queer, or resource poor), carry the stigma of sin in a way that Black men do not. As a result, many of us (even those outside of mainstream faith traditions) approach our lives believing that we are flawed and evil at our core (mostly because of what our bodies "make" grown men do). What would happen if, instead of continuing to internalize a lie based on white heteropatriarchal supremacy, we took a position that we are holy, divine in fact, reflecting the image and wisdom of God? What if we understood that it is separation from this knowledge that forms the basis of our internal pain and turmoil?

Black women, we must adopt this position about ourselves! Black women, as you are reading through the pages of this book, I invite you to consider not only the truth and sacredness of my words but of your own. What truths do we continue to suppress to make others around us feel comfortable? In what ways do we continually step back or step aside to accommodate others without taking into account how others have failed to accommodate us? How will we rectify these tendencies by moving, walking in the greatness that God has already said is ours?

And if you are not a Black woman but your mother is a Black woman, your partner is a Black woman, your coworker is a Black woman, your friend is a Black woman, a Black woman is running as a candidate in your city or county, you supervise, pastor, teach, or are otherwise surrounded by Black women, or you live in a world with Black women, I implore you to RESIST every tendency you have to push back or discount the words on these pages. Before you ask yourself if our testimony, our experience, or our epistemology is valid, believe that it is.

Chapter 1: In the Beginning

What if we consider the existence of multiple, intersecting beginnings that create multiple stories, multiple truths, and multiple identities? Could it be that when these beginnings, these fragments of our lives, are added together that we end up with a clearer picture of who God is and who we are?

In thinking about the concept of journeying through life, many of us automatically think of moving from point A to point B on a linear timeline. The fact of the matter is that life is not linear, but consists of various twists and turns that move us back and forth depending on the season of our lives, and the lessons we need to learn in that season.

Beginnings are opportunities to learn these lessons, take stock of what is happening in our lives, and make amends where necessary. This is what I think about when I consider the Old Testament phrase from Genesis 1, *"In the beginning."* This "beginning" that the writer picks up on shows that something is off, the world is in chaos, and things must change. However, for change to occur, the Old Testament writer had to name what was off and identify sources of the problem at hand: chaos. It was only after identifying the problem that God could call forth life.

As I reflect on my life, it has only been when I have honestly faced myself that healing has occurred. While I have had to do this facing many times, for the purposes of this book, the "beginning" that I want to identify is when I started working for the City of Minneapolis. It was this beginning that forced me to face things in myself that I had suppressed for years.

That is the beginning where the collection of poems in this chapter starts. But it is not where the collection ends. The poem "Thirteen," for example, recalls childhood memories from over twenty years ago. The poem "Spiraling" details the sense of overwhelm I felt a few weeks before the COVID-19 lockdown while trying to balance the demands of motherhood, life, work, and PhD studies.

When I initially started writing this chapter, my purpose in revealing these very raw pieces of myself was to get it all out there. I honestly wanted nothing more than to express what I was feeling, where I was starting, and leave it at that. But the pieces on the next few pages are about more than me. They are about the collective human experience, as we attempt to move from chaos to life, again and again and again.

Rock
I am crawling out from under the rock,
The rock I've been shielding myself with for years.
Self-imposed,
But that rock makes me feel safe in a world that is not.

Now I see that I have the tools to survive,
I no longer need this ancient burial stone.
It's just that it is heavy,
And worn,
And has been here so long that I sometimes forget that it still exists and is holding me back.

Even though I no longer need it,
I can't move it alone.
I need help!
Then I can rise from this Valley of Death,
Full of the Spirit,
And walk in new life.

Cliché
There is an adage,
Tell me if you have heard it before,
That claims that if you keep an elephant chained for a period of time,
It will still operate as if it is chained once it gets free.

How come I feel so much like that damn elephant?
The chains aren't there, and those that remain are frail and weak.
And the accusations that once limited me are long gone.
But I still feel imprisoned by the thoughts and opinions of others expressed through the years,
Even though no one is speaking now.

I still operate as if the stories of the past are relevant,
Projecting what others think about me onto them before they even mutter a word.

It is an exhausting mental exercise–
Projecting and assuming,
Assuming and projecting–
But I don't know how to live without the preoccupation of what is not.
The hurt is so deep in my bones,
And I don't know how to get free.

Strength
I drew attention to what I do,
And felt such deep shame.
Why do I get like this when I talk about my strengths?
And yet feel so liberated when I discuss my weaknesses?

Freedom
It was Baldwin who said that we write to get free,
And if that is the case, I've been freeing myself for nearly twelve years.

I first picked up a paper and pen to chronicle my thoughts during a troublesome time in my life. It was a source of therapy when friends and therapists were not around. And then I discovered that I was good. That me, my pen, and my paper were indestructible. That power lived in my written words that never surfaced outside of those intimate moments with my sacred tools.

And so, I kept writing,
Prolifically.
But now, I am not only searching for my freedom but the
freedom of so many others.
For little Black girls and little Black boys and the mothers
and fathers who kiss their sweet, sticky faces goodnight.
For women who work, labor, birth, cook, heal, nurse,
comfort, style, and love beyond their own hurt.
For the weary traveler—crossing land and sea to make a
better life for their family.
For the landless.
The differently abled.
Those enslaved.
For us, I write, and I won't stop until the chains around our
ankles disappear.

Thirteen

I've been holding space since I was thirteen years old,
Still a child and going through things like most children do.
I abandoned my childhood for life,
Becoming salvation for those who needed me the most.

I grew up that day,
And other days since.
Caught between wanting to just be young, free, and innocent,
Doing all the stupid things that adolescents do,
And wanting to control outcomes that were beyond my
control.

But that didn't keep me from playing God,
To bring about sanity and stability,
Safety and peace,
Not just for them,
But ultimately for me.

When I was thirteen,

I learned to hide my emotions and put my feelings aside,
I believed that it was less important that I felt sad, angry, and scared,
And more important that I attended to the emotions of others,
I became a master at settling other bodies before I attended to my own.

More than twenty years later, I still center the needs of others above mine.
Hoping that if I just say the right words, do the right things,
I could stop death,
And bring forth life instead.

It is expected of me now because it has been a role I have played so well,
So that when I push back, self-differentiate, and set boundaries,
Some folks just don't know what to do.
I suppose they will have to learn,
Because I am no longer thirteen,
And I am nobody's martyr.

shoulda woulda coulda
I used to run out back and hide between the trees,
When I heard them coming for you.
With their whip,
Where they would strip you naked to the bone,
Before they beat you sore.

I wasn't running to protect myself,
I was running to cry,
I was praying for them to not kill you,
To not allow their rage to strangle and bury you.
I am sorry that I wasn't there,
I should have protected you.

Erasure

When you labor for massa,
Toil day and night,
Losing sleep and health,
Peace of mind and sanity,
Just to produce some semblance of fruit,
And find a bit of success–

You can't expect him to praise you when you finish the job,
He won't even acknowledge that you did it.
No, in fact, he will take the work and claim he did it himself,
That he built the structure himself,
Found the solution himself,
And everyone will call him wise and all-knowing,
And will ask for his advice to their problems,
Even though it's your blood, sweat, and tears that yielded
such a bountiful harvest!

But what should you expect?
Massa is still a racist slave driver no matter how liberal he
claims to be.

Dirt
Ending up in places you don't belong.
Whoever thought you could be the source of so much
Unhappiness?

What did I ever do to you?
Have you come to disturb my peace?
Have you come to unearth its fragile state?

Dirt.
I don't know what to make of you.
I will clean you up lest you make a fool of me.

Ghosts
Nobody said a word to me as we walked through the streets
at midnight,
Or when we sat at the park 'til dusk,

Or when I hovered in the corner for hours,
Thinking I must have been dead because no one spoke my
name,
Much less looked in my direction.

And yet the conversation's expression of jubilee and
merriment was ever present,
And so I assumed I was a ghost, flying around town like
Swayze.

Demons
Exorcism.
Casting out America's demons,
That haunt and possess Black bodies,
Generation after generation.

We are not ourselves.
The demon has taken over our tongues,
We cannot speak as we used to,
Go as we used to,
Do all the things we used to do.

Possessed,
Controlled and manipulated,
Jesus cast the demon out,
So it won't torture us any longer.

Catching the Holy Ghost
In awe, I looked on week after week as they ran up and down
the aisle,
Under the influence of the Holy Ghost.

Arms flailing and feet marching in perfect step with the
organ,
Which meted out the familiar tune reserved for moments like
these.

Dancing and hollering,

Hollering and dancing,
Until the Spirit took complete control,
And they fell.

The ladies in white rushed to cover the women with white
lap cloths lest in their quest to become holy,
They became indecent by exposing themselves before the
entire church.

I looked on until the day,
I mustered enough courage to enter in and catch the Holy
Ghost myself.

And as soon as I did,
The reverend's wife grabbed my arm and told me to sit
down,
Convinced that I was faking it because I was only nine.

Censorship

We tend to dismiss genuine needs and desires in each other
as sin,
Deviant behaviors,
And sometimes unaddressed character flaws,
Reactivity.

Not because we care,
But because in dismissing someone's need,
We dismiss our responsibility to respond to it.

People longing for water and electricity in Puerto Rico get
dismissed as lazy,
Marginalized communities looking for economic jubilee get
dismissed as entitled,
Friends and family searching for connection get dismissed as
needy,
Employees looking for a little appreciation get dismissed as
ungrateful,
Wives looking for validation get dismissed as worldly,

People crying out for emotional support on Facebook get dismissed as messy.

And so, on it goes. We force those around us to depend and rely solely on God to meet their needs. Meanwhile, we continue to extract from them, expecting others to meet our own.

Rather than censoring each other,
What if we opened our hearts and our ears to better understand what we are saying—that we are all looking for love and human connection?

And by listening we will have to do more than offer prayers and well wishes,
No, listening will demand that we enter the experiences of others, take what they are saying seriously, and respond without filtering their words to make them more palatable for our sensibilities.

And perhaps this is why we don't truly listen. Listening requires sacrifice, humility, and action. It requires movement—and we would much rather stay still, unbothered, and unchallenged.

Speechless
Last night I dreamt about my great-grandmother,
A woman I had only met a few times when I was a baby.
I—a full-grown woman now—listened to her as she tried to instill wisdom in my life,
And break the curse that haunted me for years.

And then her speech got choppy,
Growing agitated she stopped speaking.
And her body started shaking,
So furiously that she fell off the couch she was resting on.

Frightened, I hurried over and hoisted her frail body up
where it belonged,
I turned my head toward the door and opened my mouth to
scream for help,
Nothing came out!
My throat closed because of fear.

I tried to scream again.
Nothing still!
And again,
This time words finally escaped.
And help came,
But it was too late,
Because her spirit, like the others, had gone on to be with the
ancestors.

And then, I woke up.
And my mind remembered all the times my mouth had tried
to speak and wasn't able to.
All the times I tried to warn,
To call for help,
To offer wisdom,
And was silenced.
Jesus, save me from the Spirit of Muteness.

Oreo

They told me I was white,
Because I did not speak like the other Black girls.
So, I stopped talking,
And learned to write instead.
I hid behind the written word,
So that no one would ever call me that again.

Spiraling

Do you ever feel as if you are losing it?
As if all the disparate pieces of your life that you have been
fighting so hard to hold on to are slipping between your

tightly clasped hands and will, in a matter of moments, shatter into a thousand little pieces on the floor?

Spiraling

You are trying so hard not to crack, not to crash and burn, not to make a fool of yourself, your family, your people. So, despite your feelings, you get up, wash your face, anoint your body with Kush oil and Shea Butter and keep it moving even though you are

Spiraling

No matter how hard you intend to move forward, the slightest incident sends you right back to the awful place you don't want to be. Kids not listening. Whole Foods not delivering the groceries you have been waiting the whole day for. Someone asking you to do one more thing even though you can barely manage what is already on your over-flowing plate. A former supervisor in your DMs threatened by the work you are now doing.

Spiraling

You are crying now. Screaming. Overcome with grief and sadness even though you are not sure why. Panicking. Anxious. You need to find some relief right now because you can't take the buildup in your chest.

Spiraling

You turn on Pandora. Musiq Soulchild reminds you how beautiful you are. India.Arie that you are divine. Lisa McClendon that you are brilliant. Janelle Monae that you are royalty regardless of how different you might be. Auntie Nina tells you you're young, gifted, and Black. Jamila Woods that you are holy as you already are. Grandmother Aretha that you are special regardless of what may have happened to

Adedayo

you. PJ Morton brings you back to yourself. The self that was spiraling. Their words remind you that you have a reservoir of resources you can pull from, that will keep you from falling into the dismal place that you are now teetering on the edge of.

So, you light some incense. Burn Frankincense and Myrrh. Pour out libations to the ancestors and sit back, allowing the gospel playing on Pandora to pour over you as you go back and forth between listening and prayer, prayer and listening. This is how you pull yourself up and out of the hole you were falling into, giving yourself a little more capacity to make it, to overcome, even as the actual obstacles standing in your way don't change.

22

Chapter 2:
Trials and Tribulations

One thing I love about reading the narratives of other Black women is seeing an image of myself reflected in their pages. When I first read Dr. Chanequa Walker-Barnes' **Too Heavy a Yoke: The Burden of Black Women and Strength,** *I felt as if someone saw me and put a name to what I was experiencing. When I read Audre Lorde's essay* **Eye to Eye: Black Women and Anger,** *I felt as if I had found someone brave enough to name the impact of colorism and homophobia on Black women's relationships with each other. Reading through anything by bell hooks, including* **Teaching to Transgress** *and* **Talking Back,** *feels as if someone is holding up a mirror to my very soul, repeating to hooks every thought that has ever crossed my mind as she takes copious notes for her next work.*

However, the reality is that these Black women do not know me—I only know them because of the works they put out into the world. The reason I identify with them has nothing to do with familiarity in terms of personal relationships, but everything to do with the fact that our experiences as Black women are very common. Not feeling seen or heard. Being overworked and underpaid. Longing for non-extractive relationships in our families and communities. Holding it down in systems that don't love us and refuse to do right by us, for the sake of those same relationships with community and family (because if we don't do it, no one else will).

The collection of poems in this chapter reflects what happens to many of us for daring to exist in a world that would rather we shut up and stay in our place—that mythical place at the intersection of racism and patriarchy where respectable Black women supposedly live. But last time I checked, that intersection is nearly empty—empty because so many of us are out here resisting in our own ways, with everything we have, refusing to be a casualty of anyone's making.

Written Word
I learned from an early age that my stories had the power to
kill,
My experiences the potential to alienate,
My perspective the ability to inflict psychological harm.

So I learned to keep quiet,
And hold my emotions to myself,
So as not to be identified as the source of someone else's
pain.

And I buried my troubles deep inside,
Locked them up in the dungeon of my heart,
Because I desperately wanted to preserve the safety of those
around me.

Until one day I couldn't hold in the pain anymore,
The pain was causing me to rot inside,
To seek affirmation in places where a Black woman could
never be affirmed.

Still,
I spoke up.
I stated my need.
Rejected and crushed just as I expected it.
Wounded. I had to move on.

Now that I had spoken, there was no way I could keep silent.

That's when I took to writing and writing healed me.
The paper and pen are a receptive audience,
They pass no judgment.
They don't shut down if the words get too much,
They don't abandon when things get too tense.
And they never invalidate my words or experiences,
As if what happened never happened.

So I kept writing,
And before long, my writing turned into theory and

intellectual prose,
Arguments pushing back against the status quo.
But in the theory, I largely took the me out of it.
It became a space to perform and not to process the pain I
faced daily living in a racist society.

Writing became unsafe,
Too judgmental,
Un-accepting and unloving,
Laborious.

But as God would have it,
I am in a place that calls out for me to process this way again.
To get to the layers of my body that hurt the most and peel
them back so I can heal.
I have turned back to the paper and pen, such familiar
friends,
I have reserved my computer for the prose, the essays, the
think pieces,
And the paper for me to be fully and completely me.
Un-judged and ever loved,
The paper that can hold my stories and the pen that can
write them.

Unafraid to go there with me,
My ride or die.
My salvation,
My strength and my song.

We Could All Get Free
Crossing land, sea, and I-94,
We found our way to a tiny little place on Sunday afternoon.
Leaving family, work, and other expectations behind,
We resolved to spend one moment to take care of ourselves.

Natural curls popping,
Melanin on fleek,
Feminine energy in that space was life-giving, healing.

Working on our core,
Relieving our stress,
Pushing into the earth our hurt,
Instead of passing it around like champagne.

Distracted, I just kept thinking if the sistas could get free
we could all get free.

Belonging
Once upon a time,
Someone told me I did not belong.
That my skin was too dark
My voice too quiet
My hair too kinky
My character too strong
My pain too intense
To fully know and feel love
To be a part of a family, a community who would appreciate
me

And while I fought hard to repudiate these lies spoken over
me,
To some extent I internalized them,
Allowing their misguided pronouncements to steer and
shape my life.

This time I declare, no more,
Today, I resist with all my being,
Every lie,
Every evil word,
Every hostile action,
That has ever compromised, or questioned,
My belongingness.

I push hard against the demons hidden deep inside,
Whenever I hear the words of yesteryear in my ear
No to self-loathing
No to feelings of self-hatred
No to isolation and self-annihilation

Yes to me
Freedom

Untitled
One of the hardest things I have ever had to endure was
losing you just as soon as I found out about you.

There wasn't enough time to love you,
Not enough time to learn your name or hear how it
resounded in my ears as I whispered for you to be still
and rest.

I was just beginning to get acquainted,
Getting used to the idea that you were there,
For you to disappear just as quickly as you came,
How do I deal with such a loss?

Solidarity: A Haiku
sometimes Black women
need to be amongst ourselves
nothing against you

sometimes we just need
presence warmth from us
nothing against you

sometimes we just need
love defined by our vision
by our desires

nothing against you
this is about self-love and
Solidarity

Resistance
Resistance looks like countering the voices in my mind that
tell me I am not good enough–
Not qualified enough,

Not loved enough,
Not beautiful, wise, or important enough.

Resistance looks like changing the tune that drones on and
on about my inadequacies,
And how I don't measure up.

Resistance looks like denouncing every lie that I told to
myself,
The burdens I placed on myself long projected by white
supremacist heteropatriarchy.

It's time I let those things go,
And put a new God-affirming identity in its place.

The thing is, I do not even know where to start–
I am missing my culture, my language, and my customs,
The things that ground me in who I am,
And point back to the person God created me to be.

How do I recover what I don't even realize exists?

Questions
Dear sister, what happened to you?
Why is your face so downcast,
And your eyes glossed over as if you suddenly awoke from a
hundred year slumber,
As you stumble into the light,
Like a fawn learning to walk for the first time?

Sweet sis, what happened?

Sister, what happened to me?
I try to recall the memories lodged deep in my brain,
And all I get are images and colors and a sense of foreboding
doom,
But I don't understand why.

Why am I so scared?
And why do I feel so dirty,
Like the woman walking around with the issue of blood for
twelve years?

We are in fact hemorrhaging.
Why sis, why?

Help us find answers to the questions we are not even asking,
Help us fill in the pieces to this puzzle that won't allow us to
put it away,
it insists on being completed today.

Process
Sometimes I must have these conversations with myself
before I engage large groups. I must talk myself down from
feelings of anxiety, and reassure myself that I can do it, or
rather, that I can go forth and hold adult conversations with
people that go deeper than their name, occupation, or
disposition around the current weather.

Sometimes I do well. I push myself, getting out there and
risking awkwardness in all the ways it may come.

And other times? I don't succeed. I am not up for the
emotional challenge, so I stay tucked away in my little corner
of the world. Stuck in the chair with the pool stick going
through it, my protective armor when I am afraid.

This is not because I don't like people. I like them just fine!

Is it because I am introverted?

No, that feels like a cop-out. I am actually not sure why. I
guess it's how I am most comfortable in the world—hidden
in plain sight. I need to do the work around exposure being
ok.

Memo
Dear Self,
You are doing ok,
You are healthy and well,
You did nothing wrong,
You have not failed,
You are loved,
You are worth it,
You are indispensable,
You are needed,
You are intelligent,
You are eloquent,
You are charming,
You are enough.

Like We Used to Do
Come on children, gather round!
Hit the floor when you hear the banging sound.
Don't fear!
We'll only make this a little game.

Like we used to do

When we were young,
Memories ringing through my ears,
Triggered as I saw your brown body lying there.

Like we used to

I never wanted this to be your reality,
I never imagined that you would rehearse the terror I experienced,
Never mind, we'll be alright.

Just like we used to

This is just a ritual passage into adulthood,
But you are only three,
And you are a three-year-old Black boy in America.

Let me not forget

Leprosy
I thought about Mother Teresa today and how she left her life
of comfort to live among the outcasts and undesirables in
India.

The untouchables,
The lepers,
The beggars,
The (dis)eased.

And I wished that someone was brave enough to reach out
and touch me,
To handle the enormity of my pain,
Without pushing or explaining it away.

Broken Mirror Revisited
i needed you to be weak
i needed you to be broken
i needed you to be the image looking into the broken mirror
bleeding and crying and hurt

i needed you to take on the role
so i would not have to
i couldn't bear to face my own demons
so i overemphasized yours
thinking it would make me feel better

it didn't

as i have matured over the years
gained more wisdom
faced a few more challenges
i had to come face-to-face with the reality i ran away from for
years
the image looking into the gaze of the broken mirror is not
you

it's me

it's me who is broken and hurt
it's me who has been wounded and left destitute
it is me who is bleeding and crying and lying curled up on the
floor
surrounded by the pieces of shattered glass that threaten to
pierce me more

the wonderful thing is that now that i know
i can take care of the wounded little girl who bears my image
carries my name
holds my memories
and my shame

and i can set you free
from my obsessive need for you to be
my stooge

Fear
Deep down I don't think we are jealous of each other,
Afraid of our image,
Or that of our brothers and sisters.

Deep down I think we are petrified of what our existence
means,
In a sea of whiteness ready to swallow us whole and bury us
deep within the folds of the earth.

So we lash out at each other,
Sometimes fight, scream, and yell,
Going so far as to even kill and destroy.

Not out of hatred—because we are so disconnected from
death–
But out of fear,
That if we go too far or reach too high up, they may shoot us
down.

Cycles

You take a risk. You say to yourself, "Well, maybe this place will be safe. Maybe they will accept me for me even if they don't understand every bit of me." Testing the waters, you expose a little of yourself. Vulnerability and honesty for the sake of growth, relationships, and genuine transformation. You hold your breath and wait.

And then it happens, like you always knew it would. Words are exchanged and you wonder what just transpired. You question yourself saying, "Wait, I thought this was a place of learning and sharing, a place where a mature exchange of ideas could take place even if others did not agree with them." But the silence and distancing prove to you it's not.

Sadness sets in and it hurts like hell. Grief over something lost that was never really yours to begin with. The sentiment is familiar, and that provokes a sense of anger because the same scenario plays itself out repeatedly. No matter how careful, how polite, how accommodating, and understanding you try to be, it keeps happening.

You say to yourself, "Next time I won't. Next time I will mind my place." But don't do that. Don't let this beast, this burden, this curse of white supremacist patriarchy silence you! Even if no one is listening, refuse to be silent about your pain and oppression, refuse to be silent about the suffering of many at the hands of a few.

So, you'll move on. You won't let feelings of defeat set in. You'll keep pressing forward and try a new strategy or two. You'll take that next risk.

The cycle continues. At least it will, until you get off the damn wheel and break it.

Black Spaces

Having Black-only spaces to congregate,
Study,

Reflect,
And heal,
Is not only not optional,
But necessary in a society that continuously defames
Blackness.

Our coming together to claim and stake out what is rightfully
ours shouldn't be cause for alarm,
But jubilation,
And the singing of freedom songs,
Especially among us.

It is okay to simply exist,
And do life,
And worship among ourselves,
After all, this is what they do in Nigeria,
And nobody ever accuses them of hating the Japanese.

bearing witness
i saw what she did to them
how she threatened to sell them off if they didn't behave
how she'd hang them from the cross if they stepped out of
line
how she made them stand in the cold black night stripped of
their clothes
for which crime i am not sure

i only knew there they stood
waiting, crying, waiting
and i resolved that i would never make her mad
so she would never direct her anger toward me

All My Life
Fighting!
From the moment I was pushed out of the womb,
For air, existence, the right to live in this beautiful, Black
body.

All my life,
All thirty-seven years.
Fighting,
Resisting,
Saying no to the lies, the demons that lurk around every
corner wanting to silence me,
Which has mostly worked.

You see, I am still here,
When they said I wouldn't make it,
That I wouldn't amount to anything,
I'm still here.

Fighting for my life,
All my life.
And then I spend all my days fighting,
And it's the only tool I have.
I don't know how to do anything else but fight,
Resist,
Stand my ground,
Even in the face of things that are not threatening but are
blessings.
I guess it's easier to resist than to admit that I don't know
how to trust.

Truth Hurts
We won't get better unless we tell the complete story about
ourselves, how we've been hurt, but also how we hurt.
Sometimes, it seems like we believe that if we have been
perpetrators of violence ourselves that it somehow
invalidates our own stories of victimization.

But it doesn't.

We get to own our stories even if we have been complicit, if
not knowingly corrupt, participants in the story of another.
Both things can be true. And if we can't understand that, we
will forever look for someone else to fix our problems,
instead of looking within for our own solutions.

I wonder if we are ever gonna talk about the very things that are plaguing us, not the things done on the outside but the inside. The way we harm ourselves daily. No program can fix that. We cannot wave a magic wand over the insurmountable obstacles we put before ourselves, hoping for those obstacles to dissipate.

How long will it take for us to look at our own reflections and have the very real conversations we need to have with ourselves? About the way we kill ourselves? The way we despise and hate ourselves? The way we abandon, shame, and abuse our sisters? The way we crucify our men?
Why we still think white is right?

Crucifixion
Too afraid to die, not bold enough to live,
Walking around in a shell of a better version of me.
I once was,
And now,
Do I even exist?

No, for I am a ghost,
My will has been crushed,
Snuffed out,
And stomped upon,
So I might bear the will and desires of others.

I long for change,
Holy Mother, let this cup of damnation and hell pass,
Take the sting of pain and needless suffering away.

Breathe life into this decaying flesh,
So I can live again.

Punishment
There is no fear in love,
Perfect love drives away every sense of fear.
For fear involves punishment,
And where the fear of punishment exists, love cannot abide.

So maybe I do not love.
So afraid of punishment,
Of being chastised for saying the wrong thing, doing the
wrong thing, existing in the world the way that I do,
How am I supposed to love?

I shrink back so that my actions will not threaten,
I maintain silence to avoid wrath.
I withhold my passion, so I am not later crushed by it,
I guard my heart so that it is not trampled upon.

I fear way too much,
I try to rise above it and proactively strategize my way out of
it.
And the more I rise up, the more I receive the blows of death
into this mortal body,
Afraid to exist, but I am too young to die.

Are you listening to me God?
Because I am so afraid to move, unsure of what is next,
What do I do?
Who do I become?
How do I love my way out of this hellhole and emerge with
strength and honor?

There is no fear in love and perfect love takes away all fear,
I want to love wholly and completely, so fear of punishment
cannot stay.
How do I get over this?
How do I make it through?

Listen God!
Do not forsake me,
Come near sweet Spirit
Surround me with your presence
Give me the boldness I need to leave

Letter
Jesus, help me!

I am over here losing my ever-loving mind.
Please and thank you,
Sincerely yours

Chapter 3: Lipstick on a Pig

You already know that I started writing this book after I started working for the City of Minneapolis. What you don't know is that I started my job the day after the 2016 Presidential election. Yes, that happened.

Years prior to working for the City, I worked in multiple nonprofit organizations on social justice issues. I was thrilled to be doing this work, because honestly, I had a hard time finding churches that were. The lack of a social justice presence in the church—I initially went to school to be a minister—was one of the primary reasons that I got involved in the nonprofit sector, where I worked for nearly eight years.

In those eight years, I learned things that I never learned in seminary. Leading up the communications department in one of my last places of nonprofit employment gave me the opportunity to dig into articles, research, and other texts that were not accessible to me in school—texts that critically examined the persistent, racialized violence that was driving disparities in housing, health care, education, and more.

One of the thought leaders that I became familiar with during this season of my life was Derrick Bell, the founder of Critical Race Theory (CRT). Initially applied to law, and then later to the field of education, CRT asserts that racism is a permanent structure, or essence, of the United States—it is not an aberration or accidental. Because it is permanent, Bell suggests that the best thing those who are committed to dismantling injustice can do is continue to put pressure on the system to change, recognizing that systems only change (or appear to change) when the interests of those who are being oppressed converges with the interests of those who are in power. In his article reflecting on the history and impact of *Brown vs. Board of Education*, Bell gives a clear example of this, stating:

> *"Brown was not a revolutionary decision. Rather, it is the definitive example that the interest of blacks in achieving racial justice is accommodated only when and for so long as policymakers find that the interest of blacks converges with the political and economic interests of whites. Black people have been challenging segregation in the public schools since 1850 - for the most part without success. As Professor Mary Dudziak has convincingly argued, the Brown decision advanced U.S. interests because racial segregation was hampering the United States in the Cold War with communist nations and undermining U.S. efforts to combat subversion at home (2004, p. 1056)."*

Affirming this, Malcolm Gladwell's podcast "Miss Buchanan's Period of Adjustment," in season two of *Revisionist History*, states that in the decision to integrate public schools the Supreme Court twisted the words of the parents who initially sued the school district. Parents like Leola and Oliver Brown, the family for whom the lawsuit is named, took issue with the fact that they were not able to enroll their daughter in any school of their choosing. While they attested to the quality and vibrancy of the schooling that their daughter was receiving at the Black-only school, they would have preferred to enroll her in the white-only school because it was closer. So the central issue of the Supreme Court case, for the Browns, was more a matter of proximity and principle than anything else. *"Teachers were fantastic, we got a fantastic education there . . . more like an extended family, like mothers and so forth because they took an interest in you."*

Unfortunately, the Supreme Court twisted their words by suggesting that segregation in public schools was wrong because Black people were psychologically inferior. Quoting from the ruling, Gladwell says,

"Segregation of white and colored children in public schools has a detrimental effect upon the colored children . . . the act of educating Black children separately from white children caused harm. Serious harm. Segregation . . . has a tendency to retard the educational and mental development of Negro students."

As a result of the way the court demonized Black people, Black children bore the brunt of integration. It was Black children who were forced into white schools and forced to navigate violence. And at least half of the Black teachers lost their jobs because the court—along with the school district—saw them as inferior. When the Black teachers who lost their jobs appealed to the school board and then the Supreme Court—the same court that ruled in favor of *Brown vs. Board of Education*—over the matter, they were told that they were inferior to white teachers or that "they were too uppity."

Brown, then, had nothing to do with ending segregation or promoting true equality among students. Instead, it could be argued that *Brown* was more about advancing the interests of the United States as the country navigated the tension of the Cold War. An article from Reuters affirms this, stating

"The Truman administration recognized (the advantages of Brown) in the early 1950s, when it filed a friend of the court brief with the Supreme Court in December 1952, calling for the result that the court announced 17 months later. The Truman administration's brief was highly unusual because of its heavy emphasis on foreign-policy considerations in a case ostensibly about domestic issues. Of the seven pages covering 'the interest of the United States,' five focused on the way school segregation hurt the United States in the Cold War competition for the friendship and allegiance of non-white peoples in countries then gaining independence from colonial rule (Neier, 2014)."

What this all proves is that *Brown* is nothing more than an example of Bell's interest convergence. While appearing to do something to advance the cause of racial justice, Brown undermined the efficacy of Black families for the purpose of deceiving countries (full of Black and Brown people) who were finally breaking free from the grips of colonization, even as they compromised the success of these countries (which is another story entirely).

Unfortunately, throughout my time working in nonprofits and in the public sector, I have found more examples of interest convergence than I would like to admit. While well-meaning, the notion of equity as a model to grow and stabilize our economy feels like a neoliberal example of interest convergence when applied by institutions that don't care about Black people, but are most concerned about the bottom line.

I saw examples of this before the 2016 election. But I dismissed my convictions because I thought I was maybe being too critical and pessimistic. However, the election confirmed in my heart what I knew was true for a long time:

so-called liberal, progressive politics are not more racially just than regressive, conservative ones. In fact, liberal ideologies exist on the same continuum as conservative ones, as both are committed to maintaining white supremacy and upholding capitalism. The difference is that conservative politics are upfront in showcasing racial bias, hostility, and violence—and have done so even more in the last several years with the increase of hate crimes and dehumanizing rhetoric. Liberal and progressive politics do not do this, but instead, try to woo Black people through verbal commitments to support diversity, equity, and inclusion; community engagement committees; and commission reports that promise to bring about transformative solutions. Despite the money, time, and human resources invested in these efforts, things remain the same because of institutional commitments to holding power and protecting the interests of white supremacy.

In the collection of poems found in this chapter, I am committed to honestly naming not only my discontent but my frustration in continuing to protect liberal ideologies. I am committed to exposing the farce, the wizard behind the curtain controlling everyone's lives regardless of whether that wizard is a Republican or Democrat. Because evil is evil regardless of the political party affiliation, and pigs are still pigs, even if they have lipstick on.

The Lie of White Supremacy
They thought it was about Blackness,
That we were the root of America's problem,
That if we just went away or at least stayed in our place,
That America would get free.

Little did they know that the "Negro problem" had nothing to do with us,
That the problem was actually a manifestation of the disconnect among the elite and the poor among themselves.
How awful it must be to loathe oneself so much that one

would have to invent another self to channel that internal
rage!

Politicians and people in high places know this well,
When the moment is right, they prey on the insecurities of
the poor to manipulate outcomes for their own financial gain.
Caring neither for the Negro or poor whites that use white
supremacy to silence the Negro,
The United States just wants to get paid.
This is the country's oldest form of chicanery,
When will it go away?

I tell you when it will leave,
When the white supremacist finally gets free,
Healed, delivered, with their internal trauma finally resolved.

Then those at the top will no longer be able to play us,
And we can fight against the greed and corruption that have
manipulated our lives,
Together.

The Worst Among Us?
#45 is not an aberrant manifestation of the United States,
in fact he characterizes it.

he's not the worst,
he's the norm.

flip-flopping political positions when the former no longer is
convenient,
you can miss me with that liberal charade.
because he used to be one of you,
until it became clear that progressivism was not the path to
victory.

but that's exactly how politics works.
it is not about what is good for the many,
but for the system.
that is why #45 is not an aberration

he is a constant
in the lewdest possible way

Drunken Lament
I woke up that Wednesday morning feeling lost and
confused, remorseful over the events of the night before. So
much shame and a deep feeling of regret filled my chest,
compromising the air circulating in my lungs trying to keep
me alive. My head ached, my body was sore, and I wanted to
vomit up the evils that threatened to overtake the dark
skinned body that I inhabit, telling me I don't belong.

For years, I have felt this though in less subtle ways. Being a
product of the eighties, my grandmother's realities were not
my own. After all, I have always lived in the "progressive"
North and was born after monumental civil rights legislation
was passed. But racism has always been part and parcel of
my life's experience, whether I lived in the 'hood or the
'burbs. Mass incarceration. Rodney King. Massive
unemployment. Displacement and gentrification. War on
drugs. Police brutality. And discrimination. These are all
daily realities of living in this Black body, in this country that
claims to love God so much while it despises God's very
creation.

But Wednesday, Wednesday the day after that night, which
we had all been dreading for over eighteen months,
materialized what I have always feared. It made the covert
nature of racism more overt as the nation elected a fascist,
white supremacist for president. This man was clear about
his intentions for people that represented any difference
from the cisgendered white male identity, you know—Black,
American Indians, Asian Pacific Islanders, Queer and Gender
Nonconforming folks.

And they salivated for it, no matter how much we tried to
reason. They ignored our pleas and appeals to the higher
consciousness, morality, and righteousness. They lusted so

45

much for the power of days gone by when it was okay to call people the N-word in one moment and lynch them in the next. They craved the freedom that comes with male patriarchy and treating women as sex objects with no personal ideas and inclinations. To them, this was liberation, they only felt secure in their humanity when they stripped others of theirs. They denied the image of God in people who look like me, insisting that in a world of seven billion people theirs were the only lives who truly mattered. So they refused the call of the prophets and priests among us, quenching the spirit of God begging to break forth in themselves in order to satisfy their depraved desires.

So now. We grieve. We lament. We the Black ones whose lives are already under attack every single day. We the American Indian ones who are fighting to hold on to the last bit of land we have and save our earth. We the undocumented ones—Asian, Latino, African, and Caribbean—who fear instant deportation, whose children are too scared to go to school, who are afraid to even contemplate what it is to go back to our own countries of origin that have been decimated through US foreign policy, trade, and war. We the queer ones, whose bodies people just won't allow to exist. We the Muslims who've been called unworthy, who've been labeled terrorists, who are stopped and profiled before we even leave our homes. We the women, who already experience assault, whose bodies are already over sexualized, whose voices are already silenced because no one dares to believe our stories are real.

We are the voices calling out from the margins denouncing America's sin. We weep because you have chosen the fleeting pleasures of whiteness over our existence. We wail because you used religion to cover up your hatred of us, insisting that this was about God when in fact, you denied him over and over again. We shake our fists in rage, fearing what may happen, agonizing over what has already happened to our babies, our folks, and our kin.

And yet.

We forgive you. Therefore, we will resist you. Our collective liberation is tied to our resistance of this great evil that eats at the soul of our nation.

We love you. Therefore, we will rebuke you. For if we do not rebuke, we do not love.

We wish to be at peace with you. And we will protest you. We will shut down freeways. Disrupt your meetings. Disobey your laws in order to get through to you. For true peace cannot occur without a prophetic telling of our pain and suffering. If Christ could not reconcile us to God without calling us into repentance, without disrupting systems of oppression that compromised Black and Brown bodies in His day, expect nothing less from us. We call, no we implore you to be delivered from the sin of white supremacy that steals our land, kills our bodies, rapes our women, and denies our sons and daughters the opportunity to be free.

In our liberation, you will find deliverance.

In our liberation, you will find deliverance.

In our liberation, you will find deliverance.

Dear Allies
I do not know what your role will be once I get free.
I suppose you could take up knitting,
Start a garden,
Read a book,
Travel,
Take a long luxurious walk,
Find Waldo,
Follow the Yellow Brick Road,
Or do several outstanding or very mundane things.

I don't know!
I guess I am not sure
what your calling will be once I am fully and completely
liberated,
And I am not sure how you can best serve me on that path to
my freedom,
freedom that is self-defined—and not imposed.
Your question shows that your identity is tied to my
oppression,
And that you may just be in this to make yourself feel useful,
relevant perhaps, at my expense.

Shame,
I thought you were here because of our shared humanity.

P.S. Once I get free, and I will, don't go setting up some
mission in Africa or South America, trying to "help" some
people group get "civilized." They also don't need your
allyship.

Feminism?
White women,
I will never understand why you felt more affinity for
someone who objectified you,
Dragged your holy name through the dirt,
And colonized your body,
Than you did for me.

I can only assume,
That this was never about the rights of all women,
But the liberties of white women.
Pity.
At least we now have an understanding.

And just so we are clear,
Please don't come over here asking about no allyship

Evil
This world is ruthless and heartless.

It will chew you up,
Spit you out,
And then chastise you when you resist.

Breathe
I can't breathe,
Your unrealistic expectations are suffocating me.
But you can't hear my cries for help,
Over the noise of your ego.
Maybe you think my existence clashes with your own,
But I don't need to die,
So that you can live.

Cecil
Isn't it ironic,
That the same people who have stripped a continent of its
people,
Its resources and its land,
Would be so enraged over the death of a lion?

For that lion you marched,
You protested,
You wrote letters,
You shamed others,
While not giving two shits about the people who lost their
lives in the Middle Passage.

The ones forced to labor against their will,
The ones currently starving and destitute because of
America's obsession with oil, diamonds, and chocolate,
The ones trafficked and victimized daily.
Your priorities are misplaced if you care more about Africa's
majestic lion,
Than you do Africa's magnificent people.

Babel
Babel went up in flames,
I cared not that it burned.

I watched on in delight as the twin flames of blue and gold
consumed everything in their paths.

One by one the strongholds fell.
One by one, they loosened their grip
Over the lives of the people as they disintegrated into ash
and dust piling up on the earth.
Reeking not of smoke,
But of the death it had harbored within its walls.

Babel fell today!
That great untouchable city became nothing in a manner of
moments.
And they asked us if we missed it,
And chastised us for dismantling it,
As if Babel were our best hope at salvation.
Oblivious, or perhaps, not even concerned that for all of its
glitz and glam, it thrived because our blood gave it life.

Today, Babel came tumbling down,
And we were the ones who broke down the walls.
We were the ones who lit the flame in its sacred places,
Who tore through the fortified walls with our nails.
Unbothered by how the flames might have torched us,
Unconcerned with the blood dripping down our fingers.
We were going out free today,
By every means necessary.

Chaplains of Destruction
Here we are doing the best we can
Giving all we have
Laboring day in and day out
Sleepless nights
Restless days
Heartburn and indigestion
Fatigue and burnout
Trauma upon trauma inflicted upon our mortal bodies as we
stand with arms straight up, trying to keep the sky from
falling

But the foundation is crumbling
In fear, it wages war against anything and everything that
challenges its authority
Pretending to be Oz but we done looked behind the edifice a
long time ago
There is no wizard
No greatness
No magic
About its being

Like a virus, it feeds on others
Black fathers and sons
Small immigrant children
The land and the sea
It continues to consolidate power
Grasping for whatever it can reach
Taunting those who don't realize that for all it purports to be,
It has no clothes
And it is dying

Dying a slow and painful death like all the "greats" before it
Becoming a nonentity
An afterthought
An embarrassment for all those that live in its borders
A laughingstock to all those who live without

Old and senile
It's beyond decay
It continues to suck air but it can't even breathe on its own
That's why they slay us, that's why they cut us down
Confusing us with Jesus, they think our blood will save it

We think we can save it
Perhaps if we adjust our strategies, change up our tactics, we
can keep the walls from closing in
So we fight and resist,
Not for our liberation
For its preservation

Failing to realize that at a moment's notice it will dispose of
us as it disposed of them

Don't get me wrong, we are all well-intentioned
We hope against hope that our work, our projects, our
committee meetings, and our prayers can change things
And that our efforts might keep this beast on life-support a
little while longer
But trust, the day is coming when all the breath will go out of
its body
And nothing will save it

Not equity
Not diversity
Not inclusion
Not policy reform
Not the democrats and definitely not the republicans
Not all the well-intentioned people
Not the dispossessed people

Babylon is falling
And we can't save it
That magnificent city is crumbling at its core
And we can't prop it back up
But we can save ourselves
And our children
And our family
And our community
This thing is dying
We can't set our hope on its reformation

The death angel is at the door
It's about to cross over into eternal damnation
Not paradise, not with all the blood on its hands
The bodies it has crucified testify against it
Will we do so too?
Or will we continue to nurse what is already dead?

I can hear the bagpipes playing in the distance. The mourners are lining up on the streets, trailing behind the hearse. They scream and grit their teeth in disbelief because this is where they placed their hope.

But there is no salvation here
That which has robbed so many lives cannot give it
The things that have caused so much war and pain are in no position to extend peace
But don't you worry
Those whose bones are buried beneath its foundations will come back to life
And mothers will reunite with their sons
Fathers will come home and daughters will sing for joy
Land will be restored to its rightful owners, the sea will once again give life
And the holy waters of Heaven will flow as they did in the beginning
And we will live again as the empire lives permanently under our feet

Charleston
Your oppressors forced you to carry a cross,
That they fashioned with their own hands,
That killed your loved ones and would eventually claim you.
They made you say, "Father forgive them, they know not what they do,"
As they mocked and spat upon you,
And persisted in nailing you to that wretched dogwood.
Every word you spoke in that moment was precious.

We knew that life was leaving you.
The more you tried to grasp it, the quicker it left.
You did not understand that the confession would not buy you any more time.
And that soon enough, the oppressors would succeed in their task.
Guilt free.

Four hundred years of oppression and pain bubbled to the surface as you lay dying,
Suffocating under the weight of conquest, slavery, murder, and Jim Crow.
You became the scapegoat for a nation that did not want to be saved.
They only wanted absolution!
I mourned for us that day.

Sacred Duplicity
America!
The proverbial land flowing with milk and honey,
Cookie cutter of Rome's eternal city,
God's dwelling place now that the temple has been destroyed,
Anointed and chosen,
To wreak havoc upon the earth.

You defame the name of God,
The way you treat God's people.
Stealing some, killing others, marginalizing all,
For the sake of your sacred dollar.

The annals of history are full,
With the names and faces who you have battered to have your own way.
Escaping your own hell,
You've created it for others.

No need for seven years of tribulation,
Evil is alive and well right here.
You exonerate yourselves with pious language,
Hiding behind pretentious platitudes and prayers.
As if God would look past your misdeeds of racism and white supremacy if you put His name on it,
As if God wouldn't care about the stolen lands and stolen bodies,
And hungry bellies,

And polluted waters,
If you shouted and danced hard enough,
Like the prophets of Baal.

But God can't hear you over the harrowing screams of Black
and Brown folks,
Whose sons and daughters lay dead in the streets,
And whose mothers they cannot afford to feed,
And whose fathers are dying because they don't have health
insurance,
And whose family is being deported unless #45 gets his wall,
And whose sisters and brothers and play cousins live under
the constant threat of death and destruction because their
very bodies testify against the misdeeds of a country that
claims to love God so much while hating God's people.

And still you have the sheer audacity to get upset when we
grow indignant,
When football players take a knee,
When we march through the streets chanting and screaming
And burn down your cities.

You come up out of yourselves when we block freeways,
Call us thugs when we shut down malls,
Shoot rubber bullets at us when we protest your building
projects,
Arrest us when we break your racist laws.
As if we should take the violence,
And constant degradation,
And just roll over,
And let massa hit us once more.

As if silence is more godly than resistance,
As if being complacent will get us closer to freedom than
demanding liberation.

America, not beautiful,
You have always been hell to me.

We see through your ruse and find you wanting,
We see through the lies and find you deeply scarred.

Won't you consider for just a moment,
God's imminent judgment.
Won't you repent,
Put on sackcloth and ashes,
Tarry all night long on the altar,
And lament over all that you have done?

Won't you turn from your evil ways,
And loose the chains of slavery that you have been holding
onto so tightly,
And make amends with those you have destroyed,
And provide food, housing, and water to those you have
ripped off?

This is what repentance looks like.
This is what religion consists of.
This is the sacrifice that pleases God.
Everything else is an act of duplicity.

A Prayer for Resilience
Hold us this day, God, hold us
As they release this footage of how they shot our brother
down for simply existing
For breathing while Black

Hold us

Console us this day, God, console us
As we cry tears of unbearable grief
As our hearts get ripped out of our chest, again
Console us

Sustain us this day, God, sustain us
In their arrogance and wickedness, they taunt us
and they laugh and make a mockery of our pain, relentlessly

so
Sustain us

Keep us from falling apart
Keep us from surrendering
From resigning
From letting go
So many times we want to let go

God,
Stay with us
Be our refuge
Be our rock
Fortify us
Keep us
Save us
Save us
Save us
Save us

Today God!
Not tomorrow
Not next year
Not in the next generation
But today

Kente
You must have really thought you were doing something
Dressed in our symbols of liberation
You must have really thought you could easily put it on
Adorn yourself in our garments

You must have thought that we would applaud and champion
your efforts
Think you were really down for the cause
And committed to the end of our oppression
As you kneeled in the halls of power

Check in with Katy and Taylor (and Miley and Kim)
They will tell you we do not like it when you try to be like us
We do not think it is cute, funny, or trendy, when you take
things that are sacred to us and use them for your own gain
Like winning the next election

I know that you were trying
Trying to show us, and the world, that you are in solidarity
with Black lives
And that you won't tolerate white supremacist violence–
whether at the hands of a cop or some self-appointed
vigilante
At least this is what I hope!

But rather than performative gestures like these
I'd prefer you pass an actual policy that gives us the
assurance that there will never be another George Floyd, or
Breonna Taylor, or Tony McDade
That sentences cops that assault and take Black life
And moves beyond calls for police reform that do nothing
And return the Kente cloth to its rightful owner
It doesn't belong on your necks
Not after four hundred years of your knees being on ours

Chapter 4: Holding up the World (Even as the World Kills Us)

"I saw God in myself, and I loved her fiercely." In all of literature, this line from Ntozake Shange's **For Colored Girls When the Rainbow is Enuf** *speaks the most deeply to me. The notion that I as a Black woman could embody the Divine was a radical idea, considering that from a young age society taught me there was nothing holy about women and especially not Black women.*

From a young age I recognized that in the church, Black women were seen as Jezebels unless we were chaste, dressed in a certain way, and remained quiet. Outside of the church walls, I understood that we were often viewed as too angry and so strong that our own men didn't even want us (especially if we were opinionated, educated, or financially independent). It was not until I became an adult that I began to understand that these stereotypes serve as the basis for our oppression, with our own bodies to blame for the sexual and physical violence we continue to endure.

How can something that is Divine also be the source of so much evil? As Delores Williams teaches us, the evil is not produced from inside of us, but comes from without. What white supremacist patriarchy does to the Black female body has no bearing on our relationship or connectivity to the Divine. However, when we grow up in spaces that are not affirmative of our identity—as I did—we quickly internalize the lie that God cannot ever be pleased with us because of what our bodies cause men to do to us or because we have reclaimed a semblance of sexual pleasure for ourselves.

Despite what has happened to us, there is something immensely sacred about the female stuff we are made of. There is something about our bodies, not just our spirits, that reflects the very essence of God. For me, that essence is the ability to create and sustain life. In the same way that the Spirit of God created and sustained life through the breath—as seen in Genesis 1 and Ezekiel 37—our bodies do the same, whether we are natural mothers or not.

It is not lost on me that the bodily organs responsible for sustaining the world are demonized and sexualized. It is not lost on me that reproductive decisions that should be ours alone are the basis for political pandering by both the right and the left. It is not lost on me that men who cannot create and sustain life in the same way—they have neither wombs nor milk-producing breasts last time I checked—are the very ones who exert authority over females who do. Wherein our life-giving capabilities should be a gift to the world, they are either demanded from us or are in some cases denied, which is the case for women—mostly women of color—who have been sterilized against our will.

But it is not just what we produce through our wombs that has been exploited; what we produce through our labor and our hands has been extracted as well. We mother, oftentimes against our will, grown-ass people who are either not willing or not able to give life themselves. Every Black woman who has ever worked inside of higher education, government, nonprofit, health care, the public sector, and so many other institutions, particularly on diversity, equity, and inclusion (DEI) initiatives, knows exactly what I am saying here. Our contributions are simultaneously invalidated and extracted as those who are in positions of leadership over us outright refuse to address harm and pursue authentic change. As Tatiana McInnis states in her farewell letter to DEI work, we are hemorrhaging because of the continual lack of regard.

Our bodies, our intellect, our very essence is a gift to the world. I do believe the world knows this. But rather than validate the gift, or treat the gift appropriately, white supremacist heteropatriarchy causes people to believe that the gift is meaningless, even as they demand more and more from us. What if, rather than extraction and exploitation, the gift bound up in the bodies of Black women was validated, cherished, and respected? What if instead of denying the Divine in Black women out of jealousy and competition—let's just be honest—the world asked what God wants to convey through our bodies that God cannot convey otherwise? This is what the collection of poems are about in this chapter, calling out our tendency to hold up the world even as the world continues to harm us.

Angry Black Woman

How should I compose myself?
Now that you have killed my children, raped my mother, and beat me beyond recognition?

You force me to live in dilapidated housing conditions,
Where the rent is higher than a two bedroom in the suburbs.
Yet you pay me less than the minimum wage, and threaten to take that if I complain
I am only of value to you with my tail high in the air
So I bend over and twerk some more, even though I am tired and my feet are sore

How should I compose myself?
Now that you have taken my loves and denied me my God-given liberty?
I will put on a smile and laugh with my head pulled way back,
Like those high society girls who pretend as if they don't have a care in the world
Knowing that my anger is powerful enough to destroy

I will not bury this godly rage on the inside of me
I refuse to keep silent about it any longer
But I know that you are afraid of my anger
You are afraid of my righteous indignation
You are afraid that what you have done to me, I will do to you
You fail to understand the power dynamics in this complex

relationship of ours
You have the military, the police, and congress behind you
And all I have is my God, my hands, and a multitude of voices
standing with me

And so with my hands, I will go to my God
Who can handle my anger,
Who won't force me to be silent
Who listens intently to my cries,
And will deal with my oppressors in time

And I will raise my voice along with the multitude of other
voices centering Black liberation
Refusing to be silent about our oppression to make others
comfortable
Even if in so doing, it makes us look angry

Zipporah
ebony-colored skin that matched the dark of the night
her hair, the kinky curly type
twisted up, out of her face
adorned with a scarf to keep the flyaway curls from falling
back in

garments of royalty clothed her petite body
colors of purple, ruby, emerald, and gold
reflected off of her already rich skin
brass bangles that her father made for her
clinked together as she walked
making an even louder sound as she chased her small
children through the arid land

pursed lips, hips wide, smile bright, and her heart even
brighter
hated only because the rays of the sun bounced off her
beautiful Black skin, blinding others who only wished they
could stand out like so

God took care of her dissenters, those who mocked and
laughed as she walked by
those who called her ugly as she smiled, those who said that
she just needed to sit down and mind her place as she spoke
from the depths of ancestral wisdom they themselves did not
possess
or had long ignored

that Blackness that other women despise and men secretly
covet makes the world go round (though no one would ever
tell you so)
this Blackness birthed in the richness of the Nile river delta,
where the Sun is bright, and the soil is succulent, and the
bounty of life is as present as it was when God commanded
the waters to be still
this Blackness is our beginning, to expel it would surely be
our end

Unsolicited
going out of her way
she openly declared how troublesome little girls were
when my daughter was standing right there

Protective
Drawing her close to my chest, I held her and comforted her
as the teacher reprimanded her for something she did not do
I wanted her to know there was safety in me and that I would
risk my very own life to protect, defend, and honor her
no applause needed—that's what mothers do for their
daughters

Our daughters
The way we talk about our daughters troubles me!
The way we disregard them,
Dishonor them,
Abuse them and then blame them when their reaction to
abuse is anything but tame.

As if it were possible to tame the rage furrowing deep inside
their beings because of generations of toxic patriarchy now
marked on their DNA, carrying around the scars as if they are
perpetual crosses that they must take to the grave.

No, the way we talk about our daughters frightens me!
The way we cast them aside in favor of our sons, the way we
demand perfection when they, like us, are perfectly imperfect
human beings and brilliant.
The way we insist they grow up and behave like adults, to
take care of actual adults, when they are still children.

The way we place on them the yoke of these damned gender
roles, curses that we ourselves cannot carry and yet we insist
that they fulfill their duty and fall in line with a paradigm that
will suffocate them and be the death of their dreams.

We love our sons because they are free from this burden so
they move about the world less constrained,
But our daughters carry the yoke right out of the womb.
No wonder they are a little feisty, they are resisting all of the
norms we keep trying to put on them.

And they will resist until they see no other way and will fall
in line like the rest of us,
Marching to the tune of the unhinged male ego and the
unchecked internalized patriarchy that lives inside of us.

Why do we despise them so?
Why do we loathe our daughters when we should be fighting
for them?
We should be fighting not just to break the ceiling but to
destroy the whole damned yoke of oppression that threatens
us all so that our daughters, our babies can fly freely.

How Long?
You know
It wasn't your fault
You did absolutely nothing to bring on the violence leveled
against your body
It wasn't anything you said
How you looked
Or how you acted

But you feel like it was, so you adjust
You take back the boundaries you tried to set
You reassure them you are okay even though you are boiling
on the inside and bleeding on the out
You go along to get along, attempting to smooth things over
so that the violence doesn't happen again
Or so it doesn't get worse

You coddle
You protect
But it is eating away at you
And you are sacrificing your sense of well-being because you
are too afraid of what lies on the other side of the *what-ifs*
On the other side of this intense pain if you lean into it
Instead of pretending it doesn't exist

Know this: You deserve better than this
You deserve the world
You deserve peace and joy and happiness and love
Genuine love that will never ever make you feel as if it is you
Genuine love that respects your no whether you have been
dating for one minute or married for fifty years
Genuine love that will never threaten you into submission
And make you feel as if you are losing your mind
As if the stories you tell yourself are only that—stories
Mere figments of your depraved imagination

One day, I hope you find that love
The love your heart longs for

The love you were created for
One day, I hope that if your situation does not change
That you can leave
In peace

John 8
Through the flood of tears streaming down my face, I caught
a glimpse of what he wrote on the ground:

"My daughter, you are safe with me.
I will rescue you and defeat those who oppress you."

At once, my tears dried up and I was no longer afraid of the
accusations they threw my way–

negro, ape, jezebel, not good enough, sinner, spoiled goods,
slut, home-wrecker, too dark, too short, too black, not black
enough, not pretty enough, not eloquent, intelligent,
charismatic, enough

Brazenly, I looked my oppressors in the eye,
I knew they couldn't get me anymore though they were
armed with stone, the law, and their twisted, colonized
version of the Word of God,
Ever ready at Jesus' command to bring the full force of their
might upon my petite, feminine frame.

And then Jesus,
Just as Jesus always does,
Flipped the script and beat them at their own game.
Enraged, they put down their weapons they wished to use on
me and looked for a way to use them on Him instead

Daughters
She told me she had two daughters,
And that she didn't care for them very much.

"I love them, but I definitely don't like them."
Words spoken dismissively, matter-of-factly, coldly and
detached.
What a wicked way to treat our own,
What an awful way to hold our daughters!

I definitely wasn't going to seek parenting advice from her!

Black Woman

I am a Black woman in America, and like many other Black
women I know, I feel like the mule of the world, or rather, the
person made to carry the burden, the responsibility, the
wishes, and dreams of others with little to no
acknowledgment of the miraculous feats I manage to
perform through my worn-out soul and body—because that
is just something Black women do.

We juggle multiple jobs. Sit on committees. Take care of our
children and our parents as they age. Hold it down for family
and community. We are the sage, the spiritual guide, the
comforter, the organizer, the activist, the banker, the
administrator, the provider, and wear so many other hats.
We are trying to save all of us and rescue the babies from the
lion's mouth, told repeatedly that our sacrifice is required to
make things whole again.

But we are the only ones on the mountain with the knives to
our chest with no one around to rescue us after we have
given our all!

When we get agitated, they tell us "You need to rest." Yet, the
demands keep piling higher and higher because in the next
breath they insist they need us to turn one more trick, turn
the water into wine, but we're not Jesus and aren't anybody's
savior. Or mammy.

Still, we put in more time after we've already worked a twelve-hour day, after everyone else is asleep knowing that rest would be nice, but this is the only time to get it done. And we know if we don't do it, it won't get done. Or the burden will just pass on to another sista so you grin and bear it, barely able to stand up under the weight of it all.

Still, we carry it, until our knees buckle, and our body breaks down. And they will call us haggard and bitter when we can no longer perform the duties assigned to us. Because a mule is only a mule. If we are not producing at the maximum level, we're deemed worthless, we're expendable, we're replaceable.

At least that is what they told us. That is what they make us believe. Truth is, we are more precious than the gold in our eyes that lights up every room we walk in. Truth is, we are more valuable than anything this world has ever seen. Truth is, we are the embodiment of the Divine, as evidenced in the way we walk, how we talk, the wisdom flowing from our being.

Truth is, we are brilliant Black women! We are nobody's mule. We are nobody's mammy. Walk in that truth.

Rationalizing
It's hard to speak up,
When you know that just as soon as you do, you will be silenced.

It's hard to stand and take a risk for something you believe in,
When you know, more often than not, you will be cut down before you have formed a complete thought.

It's hard to continuously do what is right when your every move is called into question.

But the alternative? The alternative is more gruesome than the slow death that comes from doing what is right, taking up space, or speaking up.

So, in the words of Audre Lorde, it is better to speak,
Remembering,
We were never meant to survive.

I wasn't meant to survive,
And with every breath that I breathe,
And with every word I utter, it is a reminder to a soul-sucking system that one escaped the claws of death.

No wonder they seek to put a muzzle on me,
My existence is a constant reminder that they did not win.

The Woman at the Well
The nameless woman at the well keeps coming to my mind.
Rejected by friends, family, and community,
She was essentially alone,
Isolated in a sea of others to avoid the glare of death.

And even so, Jesus invited her into discipleship. He called her to go deeper despite what others said about her, unconcerned with her past, the rumors, her reputation. He invited her in and held her close.

Finding her not only worthy but fully accepted

And sometimes, well often, I wish Jesus was right here today to advocate for me like that

Breaking Rules
the world is ruthless and will marginalize and silence women
for no reason at all, let alone when there are issues present
why is there this incessant need to silence our voices why the
obsession with perpetual exclusion and when will the world
wake up and realize that our survival necessitates bringing in
the wealth of wisdom we hold within our bodies let alone our
minds we have the capacity to change the world perhaps this
is why we are silenced hushed pushed aside and annihilated
when we've stepped out of our place the world can't handle
our glow the world cannot handle our pain so it consistently
places a lid on our light and forces us into darkness but we
refuse our death and are pushing back against the force of
white supremacist patriarchy trying to take us out when will
they realize that our collective salvation is bound up in our
collective liberation

Bitterness
We are not angry
We are not bitter
We are tired
Of being overworked and underpaid
Of giving much and receiving little
Of having to hold it together for everyone else at the expense
of ourselves
Of your tired excuses for why you are not available
Of white supremacy and patriarchy
Of All. The. Games. Every. Single. One
Of abuse
Of abandonment
Of chastisement
Of competition.

So quit the charades, let us take a nap, and we'll be good,
alright!

Double Bind
I keep trying to be like Mary and sit at the Lord's feet,
Undistracted by the needs of this world.
And yet, the world keeps pulling me back toward Martha–
Busy with mothering, caring for the home, going above and
beyond at work, doing it all at the expense of self.
And then the same world, that continues to mount the
responsibilities and criticize when they are not done, has the
nerve to suggest that I need to rest–

"Chill"
"Take a load off"
"Stop doing the most and just be"

If I could, I would have done that a long time ago, don't you
think? These boulders you place upon my shoulders are
weighing me down. How I wish I could shake free!

One day I will. 'Til then, the struggle continues—I must
continue to meet the demands of Martha while fighting
evermore to be like Mary.

Little Black Girl
I see you, sis
I see the confidence in which you walk,
I feel the energy shift the moment you walk into a room,
I hear the wisdom pouring from your life like the Niagara,
mighty and ever flowing.
Your words taste sweet like freshly baked pecan pie á la
mode with caramel drizzled on top,
And your spirit, it smells like summertime, trees, and fresh
rain.

Child, there ain't nothing wrong with you!
That smile of yours brightens the world.
And your eyes, there is healing there, you have the capacity
to change the world with your gaze.

Don't let someone else's insecurities keep you from being
you,
From tasting like pie,
And smelling like freedom,
For inviting the world to change as you look on.

See, you cannot change,
You cannot be silent,
You cannot grow weary in well doing.

Sis!
Do you hear me, child?
Do you hear me, little Black girl?
They need you and they don't even know it!

Sis! You have so much power and anointing
You've got to speak! You've got to get free! You've got to . . .

Don't let them silence you, sis. Don't let them kill your spirit.
Little Black girl!

Don't let that flicker in your eyes go out,
Don't let that fire in your heart grow cold and die,
Don't let them kill your spirit.

Guard your heart,
Speak up,
And keep moving.
We've got you!
We are all surrounding you,
And are cheering you on.

Tried It
They told me that if I was good
And didn't mess with the boys
And wore long skirts

And blouses buttoned up
And was polite
And served Jesus
And did not hang out late
And always went two-by-two
And didn't flirt
And minded the company I kept
And didn't drink, or dance, or do anything that could be
misconstrued as promiscuous
And spoke up, but not too loudly of course
And kept my legs closed
And my language clean
And my heart pure
And didn't wear my heels too high
And learned to fight
And screamed if I was being threatened
And walked along busy streets
And kept my distance
And didn't look too good
And . . .

I tried all of the ands
I even invented my own; it didn't work
It didn't stop inappropriate language from customers
It didn't keep men from practically groping me after I
preached a sermon
It didn't stop the little boys from trying to get it
It didn't persuade fathers of my peers wishing they were just
a little bit younger
It didn't prevent the older men from telling each other I was
ready
It didn't keep men—younger, older, black, white—from
asking, "When can we fuck?"
I tried all of the tricks that I could think of
And nothing could stop their advances

But I was never the problem
It was never about me

It was them all along
Maybe no one ever told them
That it just isn't polite
To harass and assault women

Setting Eve Free

Sister girl, how they've had your name locked up for years!
Said it was you who ate the apple,
Was led astray by your lusts.
Bringing down the integrity of the world,
With your seductive touches,
And questioning, wandering eyes.

They said it was you who've been entrapping men,
Bending and folding them in the grip of your thighs.
Tantalizing them with the fullness of your breasts,
Leading them to hell with the way the sun radiates off your
tightly curled 4C black hair,
Whether it's locked, picked out, or flowing down your back.

So, they told you to shut up!
Put up,
Dial it back,
Stay in your place,
Be seen and not heard,
And accept your plight as ordained by God for your sin.

And we believed them.
We let them drag your name through dung itself,
We distanced ourselves from you,
Disassociated ourselves from the most intimate pieces of
ourselves so that we would not also succumb to the Jezebel,
Sapphire, Delilah stereotype,

But we've gotten older and a bit wiser.
We've had children of our own, the stretch marks in places
we didn't even think were possible,

The graying of our hair while we still try to maintain our
youthful vigor of days long ago, the way our thighs jiggle now
as we move.
We've learned some things living in our bodies, being in
touch with our full selves.

And we found out they lied,
Told the biggest story of all,
And us all, believing it was you.

You who destroyed the world,
Broke up homes,
Impregnated yourself,
Knocked yourself unconscious,
Pushed yourself down the flight of stairs,
Played the whore,
Brought your misfortune upon yourself because of the way
you dressed, the way your hips moved too much, the color of
your lips, because of where you were, because of who you
were with.

Now we know,
The story is only beginning to unfold.
The truth, your truth was always here,
In plain sight in between the folds of the pages.
Though it took a trained eye to see,
Because we've internalized the lie for so long.
We needed help to be brought back to you,
Brought back to,

Our truth. The truth we bear as women.
Young and old,
Rich and poor,
Black and white and Latinx,
And Queer and,
All of us.

To see our stories, our identities so intricately wrapped
together,
Though patriarchy has damaged us,
Forced us to choose sides,
None of us are going free 'til all of us get free,
None of us are going free 'til,

Eve,
Sister girl,
Mother, daughter, friend,
From whom all living things come forth,
Who birthed the world,
Though the world despised and rejected her.

'Til Eve rises out of the pages,
Reclaims her narrative,
Tells the story that is just beginning to unfold,
To be silent no more,
To no longer be a passive or active participant in our
destruction.

The whole world is at stake,
The whole creation groans with groaning that cannot even be
uttered for our liberation.

Eve,
Sister girl.
We stand with you,
We got you,
We believe in you,
Just as much as we believe in ourselves,
In our own stories that we hold in our bodies just eager to
come out.

Love Letter (for All the Black Women)
There is something I need for us all to understand,
Something I think will help us breathe a little lighter:

A spouse is not a trophy,
Some award we get for acting right, living right.
It is not an honor bestowed only on those who've got their
shit together,
Or a stamp of approval for those who are chaste and pure,
docile and quiet.
It is not about being found worthy or ready,
Nor about being found a faithful disciple of our religion of
choice, evidenced through prayer, giving, and acts of service.

Yet we have somehow internalized the lie that these are the
things that are required to find the right one, and if we are
especially good, someone with a nice car, a good job, and who
fiercely loves their mama.

I'm not sure where the lie started,
Perhaps it's as old as slavery,
As tales were constructed, twisted, and told to objectify our
bodies and justify our oppression.
Or perhaps the lies are deeper still, finding roots in ancient
patriarchal cultures across the world in order to control our
divine, feminine energy.

Whatever the genesis, institutions are making money at our
expense.
Conferences, books, counseling sessions,
Calling in/calling out.
Sermons,
Sermons,
Oh my Lord, the sermons.
Designed to tell us to stay in our place,
Don't raise a fuss,
Be a good faithful, Black woman
And dream,
And pray,
And tithe, oh you better tithe,
And cook.

And if the sun is shining just right,
And all the stars are aligned,
You may find the right one with a shiny diamond ring,
A great big wedding,
A trophy.

I'm here to tell you, we've all been duped,
Because marriage isn't any of these things.
Marriage is an institution part and parcel to our human
existence, spanning cultures, space, and time.
It is as enduring. And it is the way many of us have decided to
cohabitate and procreate.

Now marriages across the world take different forms. There
are arranged marriages. There are polygamous marriages.
Polyandrous marriages. Common law marriages. Marriages
between men and women, men and men, women and
women, and so many other identities in between.

Despite the form, none of them exist because they had it all
together. Or because the brides were good Christian women.
No, they exist because two people came together, took a risk
on each other, and tried to make something work.

So, let's shake ourselves free of the lies we've nursed from
infancy. Put down those damned books. Stop listening to TBN
and John Gray—they only want your money anyway. And do
you, the fierce, fabulous, amazingly awesome you. Not
because you are looking for the right one. But because you
honor the God in you. And that God in you, She is lovely. She
is enough.

The Biggest Lie We Were Ever Told
They tried to get us to believe we were sinners,
That our sin and shame would bust hell wide open if we died
today.
They tried to convince us just how imperfect we were,

That even Mother Teresa in all of her brilliance and Harriet
Tubman in all of her bravery and Mama Mary in all her glory
Couldn't make it through the pearly gates,
Without atonement,
For without the shedding of blood there is no remission of
sin.

We as individuals are guilty of sin and falling short of God's
glory,
We internalize this to where we make ourselves sick.
Driving ourselves to the point of insanity to be perfect, holy,
and pure,
Meanwhile the empires that have been built by the sweat of
our brows, and the very real beatings we have taken on our
backs,
Get exalted as God's ordained mouthpiece, imbued with
Divine power to rule and to judge impartially.

But it is they that make the rules,
They who've told us just how far we've fallen,
They insist the problems of the world exist because of our
bodies,
Our blood and how it flows,
Our vaginas and how they work,

Keeping us from ever realizing that the sin of the Garden is
not the scandal,
The scandal is bound up in their quest for more power and
fame,
Glossed over with a seemingly innocent search for wisdom.

It's not wisdom they are after any more than they are after
God,
But for the sake of controlling our behavior, this is what they
pass off as gospel,
Hoping that with our continual search for perfection we will

be too busy, to distracted to look behind the curtain,
And figure out their hand.

Annotations
If you are a woman,
Further still, if you are a Black woman,
Even more so, if you are queer,
Differently abled,
Resource poor,
Or labeled at risk because you lived on 37th and Lisbon in
the nineties in Milwaukee.

If you want to be taken seriously,
If you want your words to count,
If you want to be a credible witness,

You'd best be sure to do your homework before you speak.

Before you offer an opinion,
Be sure to cross reference it.
Make sure that academic sources can verify the proof of your
words and cite scholars more learned than you.
It would be helpful if your sources were from white
researchers, and if not white, at least men. Men who have
proven to be expert researchers and thinkers on your
experience. Even though they have never been through what
you have, they are more qualified to speak because they will
be objective, neutral even, and won't exhibit emotion or
passion, in the sterilized reinterpretation of your story.

And if you are offering up historical knowledge, truth, or
wisdom that can be verified through a quick Google search,
make sure you've checked all the angles and sides of the
argument before you offer yours. Verify that the argument
you defend can be backed up by rigorous research. Make
sure the researcher is flawless and without sin so that when
you cite their work, you won't be found a fool for failing to
understand everything.

And if you are going to teach, speak, or preach yourself, be sure to do a robust literature review to ensure you understand all that has ever been said about your issue so that you can parrot the words of those who have already come before you. Caution yourself against offering something new because you may struggle to defend it. You may get blackballed, receive death threats, be ignored, silenced, or spoken over if you offer anything that has not already been confirmed by a white man and even when it is and you have done your homework and you have spoken wisely and with integrity, you will still face seemingly insurmountable challenges.

Adedayo

Chapter 5:
Remembering What We Learned to Forget

When I started my PhD program in the fall of 2018, I fully expected to leave my job with the City of Minneapolis. I was so gone. Like Monica. My anticipation revolved around the fact that until this time, my time at the City had not been an enjoyable one. I felt as if I was constantly banging my head against the wall advocating for Black people and felt punished every time I raised an opinion contrary to the ones held by the powers that be. It was unsettling going to work every day knowing that I would have to fight to exist in a system that preferred I didn't, especially if they couldn't bend my will to theirs.

But then the miraculous happened—I stayed. I still don't understand the strings that God must have pulled in the Spirit world to make that a possibility, because had I had my way, I was so gone. In staying, I was given an amazing opportunity to lead work on the City's efforts to honor the 400 Year Commemoration of Black folks in the United States.

To understand my elation here, you would have had to read my journals from back in 2014 and 2015, when I first started dreaming about what the possibilities could be to honor this sacred history. Hosting this work felt like the fulfillment of a prophetic vision, even if I didn't exactly know what "the work" would be.

Unsure of the right next steps, I started asking questions and seeking input from trusted peers and colleagues. As a result of their feedback, I put together a theoretical framework to organize all the work that would come out of this— remembering, recovering, and reimagining: *remembering who we were prior to the history of enslavement; recovering the truth about what has happened to us, including the fact that 1619 is not actually the start of Black enslavement in the British colonies;* AND *reimagining a future that is not predicated on the harm of Black bodies (or any bodies for that matter).*

I specifically channeled adrienne maree brown as I conceptualized the reimagining piece. Her call to afro-futurism and imagining a world without harm was a source of spiritual direction for me. In brown's work, I found the freedom to imagine what the City could be like in relation to Black people, a freedom that I was not afforded in my job that demanded conformity rather than innovation. In addition to brown, Gloria Anzaldua's work served as a compass. While reading Anzaldua's *Borderlands* several months prior, I was inspired by this quote, which I cut out and taped to one page of my journal, praying and dreaming about the possibilities that emerge from creativity and play:

> *"As a mestiza I have no country, my homeland cast me out; yet all countries are mine because I am every woman's sister or potential lover. (As a lesbian I have no race, my own people disclaim me; but I am all races because there is the queer of me in all races.) I am cultureless because, as a feminist, I challenge the collective cultural/religious male derived beliefs of Indo-Hispanics and Anglos; yet I am*

cultured because I am participating in the creation of yet another culture, a new story to explain the world and our participation in it, a new value system with images and symbols that connect us to each other and to the planet. Soy un amasamiento, I am an act of kneading, of uniting, and joining that not only has produced both a creature of darkness and a creature of light, but also a creature that questions the definitions of light and dark and gives them new meanings.

We are the people who leap in the dark, we are the people on the knees of the gods. In our very flesh, (r)evolution works out the clash of cultures. It makes us crazy constantly, but if the center holds, we've made some kind of evolutionary step forward. Nuestra alma el trabajo, the opus, the great alchemical work; spiritual mestizaje, a 'morphogenesis,' an inevitable unfolding. We have become the quickening serpent movement (1987, p. 102, 103)."

Months after constructing the (re)membering, (re)covering, and (re)imagining framework, I was blessed with another gift as I encountered Cynthia Dillard's theory of Endarkened Feminism. Reading her piece "Turning the Ships Around: A Case Study of (Re)Membering as Transnational Endarkened Feminist Inquiry and Praxis for Black Teachers," I literally jumped out of my skin because in her research I saw that there was a precedent for what I was imagining, and attempting to articulate. In Dillard's piece, this idea of (re)membering emerges as the endarkened feminist praxis of weaving our identities back together and reconnecting our stories of who we are in the diaspora back to stories we have long forgotten about who we were/are on the continent. Articulating the role of (re)search, Dillard writes:

> "This part of the (re)membering process involves seeking, looking, and searching for something about Black heritage and/or culture that is believed will teach us something new. In this search, we are also open to the possibly that we might be changed in this process.

Whatever we are searching for within Black identity and culture, we hope that it also helps us see ourselves more clearly—as teachers, as women, as humans (2016, p. 411)."

The more I study—through both my PhD program and self-study—the more Dillard's work resonates profoundly to me. I believe that as Black people, as Black women, we are continuously enticed—by reward and punishment—to forget our narratives. This is particularly true when it comes to the narratives of our origins, who we were prior to the *Maafa*, and the narratives of our resistance that started in Africa before any of our ancestors ever got on a ship! When we forget these important pieces, these details of our identity and history, we allow the narratives of the colonizers to become true in our thinking and reality. In pursuit of my well-being, and the well-being of everyone who looks like me, I am committed to engaging in this process of (re)membering that Dillard passionately speaks about—even as I make mistakes along the way.

The collection of poems in this chapter are dedicated to Dillard and her work, work that will continue to shape and influence my capacity to (re)connect these disparate pieces of myself, my history, and my identity. *

*The title of this chapter is named after Dillard's 2012 work, *Learning to (Re)member the Things We've Learned to Forget: Endarkened Feminisms, Spirituality, and the Sacred Nature of Research and Teaching.*

An Ode to Liberation
Liberation comes by understanding the beginning of our
story,
Not just the middle or the end.

So many of our stories begin with greatness,
Where we are from,
Who we are,
What we consist of,
Whose people we are.

To be free,
We must tap into those narratives,
And resist the temptation to start our stories now with our
oppression.

If oppression is all we have,
No matter how hard we try,
We will always see ourselves through the colonizer's eyes,
And his eyes are blinded by violence, hatred, and fear.

But if we have love,
Strength,
Innovation,
And wisdom–
If this is where our story starts,
If beauty and abundance is our beginning,
We will beat the odds,
Every single time.

Burma
I once picked up a book about the history of genocide and
violence in Burma,
And then put it down as quickly as I picked it up once I
realized that I did not know anything else about these people.

My knowledge about a group of people shouldn't be based on
a single story about their oppression,
But a complex tapestry of narratives about who they are.

Likewise, the story I rehearse about myself can't just be about what my people went through, the ugliest parts of our history,
It has to include who and what we were before the colonizers even knew our names.

Not
Not a slave
Not nappy-headed
Not uppity
Not hood
Not a sellout
Not too strong
Not a pushover
Not unqualified
Not overqualified
Not too ambitious, zealous, or religious
Not aloof
Not aggressive
Not angry
Not jezebel, mammy, nor a martyr for the cause
Not uninformed

I am not, and I refuse to be, your expectations, limitations, or vision of who you need me to be.

But you, you are also not the sum total of someone else's expectations
You are not small
Not broken
Not corrupt
Not ratchet
Not spoiled good
Not loudmouthed
Not weak or passive
Not insufficient
No

You are the embodiment of your ancestors' dreams
You are more than enough.

The Moment
The moment I stopped reacting to what others were doing to me,
Or what I thought they were doing,
Based on the stories I rehearsed in my mind,
(You know, those stories we tell ourselves about what happened that actually never happened)
That was the moment I got free.
And freedom feels too damn good to ever revert back to the internal prisons of my own making.

And if my freedom disturbs you,
The way I preach and teach,
The way I dance and sing,
The way I continually define my own reality, and redefine my boundaries,
Too bad!
Your disappointment is not a burden I am willing to carry.

Resistance
We are so busy fighting against every demon—both real and perceived,
That we miss recognizing the times we are actually winning.
Maybe it's time we change our framework from overanalyzing everything that is wrong,
And start looking for the opportunities to affirm what is right.
Even if it is less than perfect.
Our resistance will be stronger when we come to understand what it is we are actually fighting against,
And at the same time, clearly define what it is we are fighting for.

Identification
I know what it is like to be oppressed,

What it is to go without food,
What it feels like to have unstable shelter,
How embarrassing it is not to be able to afford diapers for
your newborn baby,
And have to ask your church for support,
(and they toss $150 your way only after they have proved
you've paid your tithes)
And have to go back to work less than six weeks after having
a c-section, even though your body is still open, because the
maternity leave policies are nonexistent and workplace
culture favors single men.

I know what it is like to be frightened when your husband
has been gone too long,
Calculating exactly how long it should take him to run to
Costco to get gas,
Worried as each passing second turns into minutes,
Praying that he won't turn out like the others and end up a
statistic or worse, a hashtag.

I know what it means to feel shame,
Rage,
Fear,
And despondency over every single shift in the political
landscape and national rhetoric that increasingly
marginalizes your own,
Fervently praying that the lunatics now governing in
Washington won't finally do you in,
And that the oldest member of the Supreme Court will live
long enough for this whole thing to go back to normal,
Knowing that normal, whatever that is, is not good enough
because it never really benefitted us.

I know what it's like,
Which is why I fight so hard to get free,
To liberate our people who have been hemmed up
generation after generation.

I know what it's like, which is why I write fervently,
Keep my body in shape—healthy and well—so that I can
withstand the evil directed our way.

And because I know what it's like,
I fight for you,
Sisters and brothers of all shapes and hues.
For if my liberation is bound up in your suffering,
It simply won't do.
Oppression-based freedom is an evil ruse,
All of us have to get free,
All of us must cross over the Mississippi into freedom land
together.

Because I know what oppression is like from the vantage
point of a Black Woman in these divided states,
I will fight for the undoing of your own,
Even if I have never experienced it,
Even if I don't completely know what it means to walk in
your shoes,
Even if you refuse to do the very thing for me that I insist on
doing for you,
Because we all must get free,
And we all have to cross over the Mississippi into freedom
land together.

Distractions
If they cannot keep you from shouting,
And cannot stop you from protesting,
They will go out of their way to make you feel numb,
So you no longer feel the gnawing pain inside your being that
hungers for justice, righteousness, and purity.

Once you are numb and can no longer think,
No longer feel,
No longer resist,
They will continue their activities unbothered and
unfettered,
They have succeeded in making you apathetic.

Going Home
Mother, sweet mother!
I am coming home
It has been too long since we have seen each other, greeted
each other,
Held each other and laughed.

Last time I was there,
I knew this was the place I needed to be.
I made plans to come back. Soon. But time escaped me.

First school, then marriage and kids,
Then a career, a house,
Now it seems as if I will never get there,
Back to you.

Home.

I hear your voice calling after me,
But it's been so long,
I can't understand it,
It's a shame I need an interpreter just to speak to my mother.

Sweet mother,
I am coming home.
I don't know when,
But soon, I promise.
And when I finally get there,
I plan to stay.

Sankofa
Looking back, to look forward,
Journeying through the South,
Telling our story,
In order to understand just what they did to us.
Telling the full history to make sense of our own lives.

But it is not the full story,
It's not the beginning, the middle, or the end.

It's only the last four-hundred-year narrative of a people who
have existed since God created humans,

We were there when He told Adam to name the animals
and we were there when he called Eve forth as the mother of
all living beings,
And we gave birth to civilization,
Crafting whole societies from the same dust God used to
shape our bodies.

As we look back,
Let's look back there.
Our beginning will tell us how to move forward,
The history of our ingenuity, culture, and intellect will help
us define tomorrow,
Away from our oppression,
And based on the liberation God gave to us in the beginning.

Probability
Will we get freedom on this side of glory?
Will we shake ourselves free from the chains we have carried
around on our Black bodies generation after generation?

Will we find peace and safety on this land,
With the ability to come and go and exist as full human
beings,
Endowed with the gifts allotted by our creator?

I hope and pray that we will!
But maybe,
Maybe, that's just it,
We keep looking for our salvation on the same land that
Enslaved us,
Raped us,
Killed us,
And continues to dehumanize us.

I know it's hard to conceive of other possibilities when this is
all we've known,

But maybe it's time we look to our beginning, to the land that conceived and birthed us,
For any element of freedom we hope to get in our lifetime.
For even though the blood and sweat of our ancestors built this place, it was blood and sweat that they did not give of their own volition,
And if our ancestors had the ability to do so they wouldn't have hesitated in going back home.

Ebony
Strong.
Black.
Beautiful.
Shining and valuable.
Like the trees that grow in Gabon.
Found in the tombs of Kemet long ago.

Crafted into jewelry,
And sacred symbols,
So that the possessor of those symbols would know that they were powerful because they were carrying me.

I am what my name suggests.
So rare that there can never be another like me.
Beautiful. Black. Me.
Ebony.

Living My Ancestors' Dreams
My ancestors resisted for me,
They fought for me,
They dreamed for me,
They prayed for me,
They sang for me.

And now, endowed with the ability to do even greater,
I continue the fight.
Not only for my descendants,
But for me, today.

And for my ancestors, I must heal their memories.

I refuse to wait for my liberation.
Neither do I believe that it is in some far-off future.
Liberation is right now!
Joy is right now!
Abundant life is right now!
I will accept nothing less.

The Cross
Power of God unto salvation for all who believe,
A weapon of destruction for all who don't.

Through the cross, you have liberated the dispossessed from
the bonds of hell,
And through the cross, the powerful have turned around and
put the dispossessed back in it.
Turning up the heat, it's blazing fire now ten times higher
than it ever was,
Proposing to destroy all who are subjected to it.

This beautiful cross, the blood-stained cross,
Where my Savior died to give me hope and liberty.
And still it enslaves,
It still conquers,
It still kills.

This cross, my banner
This cross, my shackles
Free me to live in the power of this broken wood,
Free me to liberate it from the hands who wish it no good,
From those who care not about the liberation of the cross,
And only care about the brutality it is able to enforce.

Will the cross ever be liberated from the chains of Western
colonization?
Or will it, like us, be ever ensnared by them?

Is it impossible to imagine that a tool of oppression could

ever be reimagined as a symbol of liberation so that we could all use that symbol to get free?

Words
The moment I put the pen to paper all my thoughts become clear,
All my fears and worries,
Hopes and dreams begin to make sense.

Without my magical tools, the world feels so untenable,
So daunting, confusing, and blurry.

Without my wand, I feel like a mumbling sycophant,
Like the Pharisees who Jesus rebuked for meaningless repetition,
I repeat, go around in circles, not because I don't know what to say,
But because I can't find the words to match the rhythm of my heart.

And perhaps, it's because my heart speaks another language that I do not have the capacity to translate,
Perhaps, my heart still speaks the tongue of my ancestors from hundreds of years ago,
It remembers the rhythmic tonal sounds of a people my mind has since forgotten.

How will I recover what is lost? How will I remember what I don't even know is there? When will I get to a place where the words on my tongue match the language of my heart?

Dream of Home
Rushing out the door, two kids in tow,
Carrying backpacks, lunch bags, water bottles, and one cup of tea for me,

Piling into the car,
Buckling the youngest one who always seems to need a boost of help to get him going,

Speeding down Larpenteur,
Praying the cops don't see me because there still is that one
ticket I didn't pay,
But I will . . . soon.

Radio is blasting, can't remember the song,
Somewhere between Lexington and 280, my mind starts to
wander to its happy place and all of the anxieties of the last
hour dissipate because I'm thinking of you . . . dreaming of
you . . . rehearsing the same dream in my mind that I have
been conjuring up for the last four years.

I started dreaming when Mike Brown was shot, and then
more when his killer got off. My dream took on new
dimensions after Charleston, intensified the more every
single time one of us fell to the ground.

The dream grew in the days, weeks, and months leading up
to the election. Expanded as the deplorables tore apart
policies my ancestors' blood paid for. Reinvigorated with
every single faux commitment to racial justice expressed by
those well-meaning liberals, and even some of us who
weren't so much interested in dismantling the master's
house as we were living in it.

No matter the cycle, the season, the news feature, the
misfortune, the dream has held steady. It has felt
unattainable, irrational, and close all at the same time. And
now, after four hundred years, it's within reach. They said we
wouldn't make it. That we wouldn't get here. But the dream
is no longer a thought, it's on the horizon. It's just beyond the
sun, just beyond where I-94 meets the streets, pushing me
out of the dream and thrusting me back into reality.

Ms. Walker, bump Canada. I'm taking mama 'em to Africa.

Target
Just so you know

There probably aren't any Targets in Wakanda
Or Walmarts
Or grocery stores
Or mini malls
Or Amazon

Most likely the people live by what their hands produce,
If they want it, they have to build it and maintain it and
patronize it,
As a community.

Not out of lack
But because of their commitment to each other which calls
for a radical economics that is not based on exploitation,
Or convenience.

How much of our convenience and comfort are we willing to
give up,
In exchange for this vision of liberation?
Or would we rather pretend we are free so we can hold on to
the spoils derived from our own oppression?

Last Bath (A Different Kind of Baptism)
We could hear you groaning,
We heard the moans and cries from miles away.
The ground spoke of your arrival,
Warned us about what was happening to you, our children.

We didn't want to believe,
We didn't think humans had the capacity to be so evil, so
hateful towards one another.

So, we mustered all the energy we could to wish, to pray the
rumors away only to be told by the ancestors that this was
happening. The best thing we could do was hold you a little
longer before the white man snatched you out of our hands
forever.

As you crossed over from the red clay beneath your feet and were thrown violently into our embrace, we clung tightly to your already battered and weary frame. We cooled you off and sang songs over you as a mother does over her inconsolable children. We didn't want to pacify you but give you the strength to keep moving if you could, resist if you had the fortitude to do so, or allow our arms to swallow you if it was just too much.

You were our children. Sons and daughters of this land. We only prayed for your well-being. We continued to ask God, the ancestors for your safety as you left our home for strange lands we didn't know. And now that you are free, we are here to welcome you back. Home. This is where you belong.

for granny
we may have left
but the spirit never left us
the ancestors have continued to guide us
separated by land and sea
they are only a whisper away

some by boat
others by plane
most through death
we all have a way of returning
of going through the door
resting on the land
our ancestors birthed us

enjoy your rest

Adedayo

Chapter 6: A Way Out of No Way

*Black women have a way of doing what needs to be done,
when it needs to be done—no questions asked. When
others have shirked responsibility, we step up to the plate.
When situations look impossible, we find solutions and
make things work. When funds are tight and we are trying
to make the ends meet, we find a way of making a dollar
out of fifteen cents.*

Like Jesus, who fed over five thousand people—not counting women and children—with two fish and five loaves of bread, we are modern day miracle workers. It's in our blood. We watched our mothers and their mothers make elaborate meals with only a few ingredients in the cupboards, looked on as they transformed barren soil into beautiful landscapes, and witnessed them work multiple jobs where they were often overqualified and underpaid to provide for their families and communities.

At least, that is my story. I watched my mother make a way out of no way to provide for both my sister and me. She did not have much help. And she did not have more than a few years of college under her belt. As a result, I saw her work tirelessly for jobs that paid her very little. And yet, there was never a time when I felt that we would do without, because she made sure that we didn't. I never remember being hungry or not having clean clothes or being worried about where I would lie down to sleep, because she made sure all of our needs were taken care of—and was really clear about making sure that my sister and I knew the distinction between needs and wants. Clean clothes were the need, but we could get those at the secondhand store. Food was the need, and you could get food at Aldi's (this was back in the day when Aldi's was terrible, I still can't stand shopping there). Transportation was the need, and so we would get from point A to B by either bus or her hoopty that often broke down mid-transit.

As a child, I never could have understood the complexity of what my mother went through in order to meet these basic needs. As a child, all I understood was that my mother was tired and kinda on the moody, anxious side most of the time. It took years into my adulthood for me to understand that without a strong social or familial network, my mother was overextended and burning both ends of the candlestick to do right by her kids.

Essentially, my mother was the epitome of the Strong Black Woman misnomer—Black women who are simultaneously heralded, punished, and exploited for their ability to be strong. We are praised because the definition of a good Black woman is to be a hardworking woman who sacrifices herself for others without complaint. We are punished because some men will use it as an excuse to not be in a relationship with us, so they are not invalidated by our headstrong, opinionated personalities. (Many years before I was married, I had a guy friend tell me that the reason that I wasn't dating was because I was too strong.) And we are exploited because every organization, committee, or religious institution that we have ever been a part of has thrived off of our acts of selflessness without fairly compensating or acknowledging us for our contributions.

As Black women, we have often tied our "choice" to show up in the world in this way to our faith, believing that it is admirable to suffer and die for the cause. But if you look around, we are the only ones dying as a result of preventable health-related causes, including childbirth, because we are overextended, and our bodies need rest. We are the ones disproportionately dying in romantic relationships—more sold out to the prospect of being faithful than being happy, safe, and alive. And if we are not dying physically, we are dying emotionally and spiritually every single day as our needs go unacknowledged and unmet by those who say they love us the most.

So rather than our sacrifice being a matter of faith, I would like to suggest that it has been a matter of survival, and we have called it faith because it feels more honorable to do something on behalf of God than because we have to. And if we are frank, we have had to be strong for the sake of our families and even our own long-term well-being. Slavery and its aftermath took from us the ability to be present with our emotions, and especially denied us the opportunity to be alive to our own needs, wants, and desires. After all these years, we still define ourselves in the context of what we do for others instead of simply breathing and existing.

In the collection of poems that follow, I raise these ideas not as an admonishment for us to necessarily put down our capes (even though we should). Instead, I raise these ideas to those who are in relationship with Black women—as lovers and friends, colleagues and more—as a challenge to enter into mutually beneficial, reciprocal relationships with us instead of continuing to extract from us. Give to the Black women in your life more than you receive from them. Pay them more. Promote them more. Quote them more. Believe them more. Love them more. Praise them more. Because you see, the Strong Black Woman misnomer is not an individual Black woman problem but a structural problem that won't go away simply by Black women learning to take better care of ourselves. Men and the institutions that serve the benefit of men need to stop demanding so much from us and do it without punishing us for taking a step back.

We deserve rest on this side of Heaven. And we deserve to put down the superwoman cape. But we cannot completely do that until those around us take on more of the work that we have been relentlessly doing for generations, without passing it unto another sista.

writing out loud
is there such a thing as balancing the call to sacrifice as a Christian with the sacrifice that already comes with being a

Black woman? or what does it mean to sacrifice when you've spent your whole life sacrificing and bearing the burdens of others because of the cross assigned to you before you were in your mother's womb based on what your ancestors were doing in 1619?

as a believer, the example of Christ admonishes me to lay down my life for others and as a Black woman, my life has never been my own—always minimized, often spoken over, seldom respected and fully embraced.

and so what is the salvation story here? if to be a Christian is a call to sacrifice, haven't we been doing that our whole lives? if my deliverance is bound up in my suffering, have I not attained deliverance that should set my children free for generations to come?

faith, then to me, must be more than the sum of my sufferings and ability to grin and bear it; it must be more promising than receiving an unquantifiable blessing in the next life as a result of my innumerable pain in this one. this is not to minimize the Savior's ability to redeem those deep moments of pain—after all, He makes all things new—but to suggest that perhaps the call to sacrifice and suffering rests more soundly on those who've done the oppressing, so that the rest of us may rest.

Glorification of Black Pain
This is a story I tried to write some years ago right after Charleston happened. Like yesterday, I remember the massacre, the faces, the names of the victims who lost their lives to hatred and racism on steroids.

As what always happens after many tragedies that occur on a national scale, the media had an interest in covering different angles of the story in hopes of gaining the upper hand in revealing something that hadn't yet come to the limelight. And one of their strategies was getting the personal narratives of the victim's families as well as the Black community to make better sense of something that was nonsensical.

"How are you feeling? What are your thoughts? Where are your think pieces and reflection on this whole ordeal?" the media and public asked, and I felt violated as they did. I felt vulnerable as people looked on waiting for answers. I felt naked and ashamed as passersby in the grocery store looked on, waiting for an answer from me as if my words could set them free from the pain and shame they felt for their violent racism.

But the moment felt too raw and unprocessed to string together an intelligible idea about the way we felt as we witnessed nine of our brothers and sisters struck down like cattle in the House of God.

I didn't want to perform. I didn't want to pump out a blog post about the trauma and rage that I was experiencing while it was still very much alive and present. The pull to remain relevant angered me the more. I just wanted to be. To exist. To heal.

Living in a voyeuristic culture where the suffering and oppression of others is constantly on display, if not even fetishized, makes such healing impossible. The pain of Black folks, studied by sociologists, anthropologists, politicians, preachers, and so many other professionals, is widely accessible, repeated, and heard so much that you have to wonder if Black suffering is a sport to some, and if not a sport, at least an opportunity for catharsis simply because they've heard the story. Does the act of hearing change things for the listener? Or is this just trauma porn?

Back to my story: Charleston reminded me of the importance of processing and grieving in spaces that affirm my identity. I can't do that in a space that strips me of my humanity or that continues to struggle over the notion that my humanity and experience is real. And so, the idea of explaining the deep anguish and suffering to a world who more so wanted a good story about that pain rather than get to the root of it felt extremely exploitative and extractive.

So, I kept quiet. Not because I didn't have anything to say. But because my grief was sacred, and I didn't want to share it with the world.

Eve
Sister Eve,
I see how they've got you all hemmed up,
Blaming the futility and shame of the world on you.

In all actuality, I think it was a set up between that conniving devil and that Adam,
who wanted to be God and wasn't satisfied with being like him.

In their lust for power, they tricked you
And placed on you—and all of us women—the burden of the sin they committed,
Justifying our perpetual dehumanization across race, place and time,
by ever "showing" us the frailty of our ways in the beginning.

Sigh

Sister Eve,
We are fighting for you,
Your liberation is intertwined with our own.
The foundation of patriarchy and gender-based violence lies in the mis-telling of your narrative,
so we are retelling it ourselves so we can get free.

Black Saviorhood

Noun

Definition: The idea that Black people can somehow save the
soul of America through sacrifice, labor, and representation

Looks like:

*Black men atoning for the sexual sins of white men through
lynching.*

*Token representation in the workplace, on committees, and in
schools, expecting the experience of one Black person to not
only represent the whole but to deliver the institution.*

*Expectations of Black people to exonerate whites for the sins
they have committed over generations. There are apologies
and cries for forgiveness, as if our forgiveness will absolve all
guilt of racism and other forms of oppression.*

Expository: The way in which Black people are continually
forced to carry the cross of racism and genocide through
historical and present-day trauma re-oppresses the already
oppressed. This is not what sacrifice is about and there is
nothing holy about it.

Black people are continuously asked to wait until the next life
to find justice, but Jesus inaugurated His kingdom here on
earth in this life, not in the next. This means that justice and
peace can be ours right here. It is not our job to save America.
Only Jesus can do that, and we as his witnesses can point to
God's saving grace, made available as people recognize their
sin, repent of it, and turn to God. And if they don't, it is not
our burden to carry. It is not our job, our role, or our
responsibility to make America see the error of its ways
because then we put ourselves in the Savior position and
become martyrs for people in problematic ways.

There is nothing innately spiritual about martyrdom.
Suffering for the Lord is honorable, but what about when you
have already spent a whole life suffering? Suffering has its
seasons—it is not supposed to endure in perpetuity. But that

is what the Black experience has been—perpetual, generational suffering and martyrdom. And that's not holy; that's abuse!

Allyship

Noun

Definition: A joke

Expository: 'Nuf said.

Equity

Noun

Definition:

1. A way for people to say something about racism and injustice by saying absolutely nothing.

2. Empty jargon that is often used by people in power to deceive African Americans, American Indians, and other marginalized communities.

Tip—it would be best if you just wiped this word from your lexicon and say what you are really trying to say.

Diversity

Noun

Definition 1: Increasing the mix of marginalized populations in an organization, constituency, staff, or board.

Definition 2: Makes people in power feel really happy that their organization is more colorful.

Tip #1: Organizations seldom implement change beyond this level though they will spend thousands of dollars to hire consultants to deliver diversity and equity training.

Tip #2: The opinion of marginalized individuals typically don't matter. Shh. Be quiet. You are just there to make the new brochure look nice.

Assumptions
5'3" with brown hair, blue eyes, and skin as white as snow, she sat down across from me. I, in my signature blue heels with my freshly twisted curls, tried to pay attention. I had already been down this road; I knew where she was going before she even opened her mouth to speak.

And then she started, explaining that she needed to remain in her powerful position in order to help people of color out instead of vigorously recruiting another to fill her shoes.

"If I am not there to open the door, write the policy, make the needs known, then how will the work ever happen?"

"Move out of the way, and I will show you," I insisted. "We can fully speak for ourselves."

"But how will they listen to you? They'd much rather hear it from someone who looks like me—that's how white supremacy works."

And she was right, they were bound to give her the floor and tune me out. I'd seen it happen before. But there was still something deeply flawed with the logic.

"Well, if you speak for me, instead of allowing me to speak for myself, won't they always be more comfortable listening to you?" I asked, taking a sip from my herbal tea that was growing cold.

"Well yes, but . . ."

"And if they are always more comfortable listening to you, you become the proxy in which they will seek validation, meaning that they will only validate my experience if you validate it first."

"Well . . ." she stammered.

"And if you are the proxy, it's no longer about me—not my voice, not my perspective, not my community, not my issues, and then we will just end up centering whiteness again. Is this not white supremacy again, no matter how well intentioned?"

"I guess, I had never thought of it like that. What would you recommend that I do," she asked?

I knew it was a trick question. I knew things just wouldn't change that easily. Yet and still, I opened my mouth to rehearse the lines I had spoken so many times before. "We need to speak for ourselves. If you are talking about racial justice and inequities, we must tell our story for our own selves. We should be your board chairs, executive directors, and lead volunteers, and not just the face you use out in public when it is time for your organization to raise money."

"This all sounds well and good, I guess. Just where does that leave me?"

Pausing, I pulled out the new Lipbar I had just picked up from Target and reapplied it. Now I knew it was time for me to leave and that the conversation wouldn't change a thing.

"Oh, there is still plenty for you to do. You can start by opening the door and setting up the table and chairs. Bring that favorite hot dish you swear by so that the people can eat. And can you watch the kids, too? That way you won't need to ask the only woman of color in your organization to babysit them. All of that would be nice. And then, you can go to your own people and do this healing work in your community."

And she thought about it for a minute. Saddened, she did not know what to do with her own self. But then she realized that it would be much easier for her to just talk to them on behalf of the community in order to save others from the hassle. It was easier that way, she insisted.

And they wonder why we fight.
They wonder why we resist so hard.
They wonder why we yell and scream and protest and insist.
And when we leave their organizations, their committees, and the metaphorical table altogether to start our own, they still have the audacity to wonder why.

Strength and Vulnerability
Why do we feel this incessant need to be strong?

What are we so afraid of by showing weakness and vulnerability, the limits of the human condition?

Do we think there is some honor attained by being stoic and refusing to let the world know when we are hurting and have needs?

Do we think we are undeserving of their care, or at least, that it is too risky to let others in?

Do we somehow feel that we will be taken advantage of?

Or are we doubtful about our self-worth?

Or is this nothing more than a learned practice, something we've internalized because the world said it made us look admirable if we suffer in silence?

But what glory is there in suffering in silence when God has given us everything we need to get better? There is nothing admirable about hypertension, diabetes, Alzheimer's, depression, or any other physical and/or mental limitation that comes as a result of feigning strength. Let's drop our cape and get the help we need today.

Tools

I wasn't created to be somebody's mule, martyr, or perpetual servant,
But I was created to hold disparate, fragmented pieces in pursuit of wholeness.
Mender of broken hearts,
Healers of wounds that have long crusted over.

Thing is, that which makes me gentle and kind for the broken,
Makes me a target to those who'd rather use this heart to perpetuate their evil.
Toughen up! But then how do I operate in grace and gentleness?

This is who I am!

The world is abrasive,
Cruel and unloving,
So many hearts have calloused over just so they can survive.
But in the pursuit of survival, we trade away our humanity.

The world doesn't need more hard hearts but gentle, rooted souls,
I want to be that soul,
And embody that healing, peaceful presence no matter the cost.
This is how we heal.

Mammy

Don't make a mammy out of me,
I really don't want to shoulder your burden and still have to carry my own.

I can offer support,
Love and prayer,

But I cannot and will not do your heavy lifting,
Your load is yours to bear.

Happiness
I learned today that my tears have the potential to make people unhappy,
What a powerful and wicked responsibility.

Happiness II
She asked me to stop crying because my tears made her uncomfortable,
Uneasy,
Miserable.

I wanted to lash out and scream that my tears had nothing to do with her happiness or the lack thereof—though using much harsher language.

Instead, I asked her to let me alone to pray for a while and that seemed to soothe her soul.

Boss Pimp
Her pimp game was strong
From New York
Big boisterous voice
The way she moved through her day at work, not on these streets, was completely
Pimpish
Maybe mafia-style

I shouldn't have been surprised when she tried to sell me out to a customer–
An elderly white man who had taken a fascination with my "exotic-looking braids" and dark skin

Panting and vocalizing his wishes as boss pimp listened intently
'You should be glad he found you desirable,' she said as I recoiled at the notion of his speech

As if the old, crusty white dude was the best that a dark
skinned Black girl like me could do

I think she missed the memo
This is the twenty-first century
We are not on some plantation
And Black women and girls are not for sale

Envy
They react so viscerally to our hairstyles,
Only because they wish they could form and conform theirs
the same way.
And I can't blame them, I mean the myriad of ways we can
comb, pluck, plait, lock, fro, twist, cut, and weave our hair one
day and still change it the next day is amazing.

I'd be a bit jealous too!

But they don't have to punish us simply because they can't
get theirs to act like ours.
Take the matter up with God,
And leave Black girls out of it.

In Order to Survive
I am not interested in changing who I am to fit inside of a
system that was not designed for me. I am not interested in
altering my personality, my style, or my clothes to be
afforded the right to work anxiously and achieve . . . what
exactly? I am not exactly sure. I guess the goal is for me to
achieve some measure of success and notoriety for
navigating the cruelty of a dehumanizing space without being
swallowed alive, even though my soul withers away daily,
right? But this does not sound appealing to me.

I am not interested in contorting my body, my mind, or my
spirit in this way. I am not interested in submitting my will
and passion to an institution that does not wish good things
for me, but that despises me and actively seeks to destroy
me.

It is a waste of time. A waste of all my best energy, all my best thoughts, all my best years to go on this way pretending that if I just perform the right way, things will change. I am not deceived; I am clear—no matter how hard I rise to the occasion, this evil continuously attempts to crush my heart and steal my breath until it subdues me.

Or makes me numb. Numb to its whims and caprices. Numb to the suffering it causes me and my people. What makes me think that just because I'm on the inside, I'm exempt from its wrath? You see, this is how we get tripped up—we think because we've arrived, we're absolved from the might of its terror. Meanwhile, the war keeps waging and rather than liberating those we said we'd help, we'll become a mouthpiece for the evil, thinking whatever good we accomplish somehow justifies our participation.

No, I'm not interested in growing numb. I'd rather be destroyed. And since destruction is not an option—I have far too much breath left in me to go out that way—I must leave. I must get out. I must liberate myself from these chains that won't ever willingly let go. And that time is now. Freedom now. Liberation now. Salvation now. Dancing and jubilation right now. Tomorrow will be too late.

Counting
How many more times do I have to say what I've been saying all along,
How many more words must I learn,
How many more concepts must be invented,
How many more degrees,
How many more tear-stained cheeks,
'Til you believe me and take my word as valid simply because I'm speaking it?

Alternatives
What's the worst that can happen if you allow me to speak?
What's the worst that can happen if you let me complete an actual sentence without jumping in with your rebuttals,

opinions, or half-baked solutions to a problem that I never
asked your advice on?

Would my words bring down mountains,
Or have the sea collapse into itself?
Would all hell break loose,
And utter chaos run amuck?

Would death become insurmountable?
Would terror and war increase?
Would my words do that much harm?
Or do you just not want to hear me?

Salvation
I wanted to rescue you from your demons,
And save you from the world.
I wanted to protect and shield you,
So that you wouldn't hurt and cry the way that you do.

I carried your burden for years,
Cried and prayed for you to get free.
Made myself crazy when you weren't getting better,
Taking it personally because I thought if I could just do more,
you could find your truth.

I set myself up to be your savior,
And maybe at some level, you did too,
Confiding in me things that only a trained therapist and Jesus
should know.
Inappropriate, I should have never had to carry this.

Always concerned and afraid for your well-being,
I never learned how to live for me.
I was too busy taking care of you,
Becoming a caregiver long before I needed to be.

Now I know that I can't carry your load anymore,
I've made myself sick and broke trying.
I carried the prospect of your loss as if I had the power to do

something about it,
But I'm not God, I didn't die on no cross; I didn't rise from the grave.
I can't be your savior,
I can't be your rescue,
Most days, I shouldn't even be your confidant!

You have to put in that work,
You have to seek the tools,
Because they are there in abundance,
And because I love you and want nothing but the best for you,
I ask that you seek them out, before it's too late.

Exhibit
I am not an exhibit
I am not an animal in a zoo
If you like what you see here
Whether it be my earrings, my clothes, or the way I do my hair

Say so politely and then move on
Do not gawk and glare
Didn't your mom tell you it's not nice to stare
And please, for the love of God, don't you dare
Get up in my face
Invade my space
In only the way colonizers do

Back up, give me some room, let me breathe!
Contrary to your opinion, I don't belong to you.
And just because you are pleased,
Stimulated perhaps, by this dark skinned African Queen as I walk across the room, or the grocery store, or down the street,
It doesn't give you permission,
To ooh and ahh like you are some damn tourist on safari in the Sahara observing the grand elephant in its natural habitat.

A simple, socially distanced compliment will do just fine,
Don't make things weird.

Caucusing
All the Black kids don't just sit together in high school
cafeterias,
Or congregate together on middle school playgrounds at
recess.
All the Black kids come together to be with one another,
In workspaces,
In churches,
In committee meetings,
In graduate level classrooms even when they are thirty-six.

Because the world without our posse feels unsafe,
Because navigating the sea of whiteness alone feels
wearisome.

*The sea that tells us you don't understand our questions when
we speak the same language.*

*The sea that grants what you feel is permission to gawk and
glare and touch our hair and then have the audacity to get in
your feelings when we insist that you not treat us like an
exhibit.*

*The sea that gives you space and privilege to be an ally because
you say the right things and rock the Black Lives Matter t-shirt
and show up at the marches and challenge white folks but your
embodiment, as displayed in your paternalistic interactions
with me, is just as problematic as the overtly racist white guy.*

So we huddle up,
Go out into the world two-by-two.
After all, your fear of us when we are many will either keep
you silent or you will walk away,
Which works in our favor.
Until you call the cops on us for what—existing together in

one space because we are trying to outnumber you so you will leave us alone and not ask us a billion questions just because you are curious.

All the Black kids keep sitting together because you have proven it is unsafe to sit alone.

Close
I always thought I had to be perfect to approach you
That I had to be on my best behavior
Mind my p's and q's
Be certain of everything I was taught about you
Never doubt and always hope

So in knowing you, I learned to fear you
Figured that with every misstep, I would be cast aside
Fall in line so that I didn't lose my place in the long line to Heaven
A place reserved only for the obedient
For the chaste, for those who fit the mold of what a good Christian girl should be

Knowing you like this felt like a burden
Instead of sugarplums, visions of hell danced in my head
Preoccupied with where I was going after I died
I stopped living, nervously trying to walk the very narrow road laid out for me
A road that at any moment I could fall off of

The day came when I finally breathed
I am not sure how or when but I finally exhaled
Perhaps it was in marching, protesting
Or in sitting in coffee shops, living rooms, and community spaces, listening to elders speak
Or in studying your Word as I engaged your world, finding that the version of you I knew wasn't you at all

For you ain't no schizophrenic for one, changing your mind about us and where we stand every second, of every

moment, or every day
Neither are you some sadistic judge, waiting to destroy us for
swearing, blasting Hip Hop or sweating out our freshly
twisted hair on the dance floor as we twerk a bit
And you are not aloof or far away, circling around the very
real chaos in our communities as a result of police violence,
hurricanes, and war, like Bush did after Hurricane Katrina

No, you are a God who is unafraid to get your hands messy
You don't hesitate to engage the worst in us while calling out
the best in us
So much so that you were unafraid to turn up at a party,
supplying wine to all the guests
That you would sit and do life with sex workers, tax
collectors, those so despised in your day that the religious
institutions cast them off as they sentenced you to death for
breaking social codes
That you would enter the homes of the (dis)eased
Let them touch you, kiss you, be so close to you that you
risked their stuff rubbing off on you
That you would descend so low as to go to where they could
not
That you would take on death, hell, and the grave face-to-
face, risking your own eternal dwelling place

A God who does all of this is not the God I became acquainted
with
A God so willing to be near and enter into all of our
messiness is not the same neurotic figment of my
imagination that I prayed to countless hours and hours,
trying to keep myself from being tainted by a world you
willingly engaged

No, you are near
You are right here
And you won't cast me off

Holy
The Spirit guides me along the right paths,

But I don't always know where I am going,
I think I understand, I think I get it,
And just as I reach to grasp it,
The Spirit shifts.

Wild and uncontrollable is She!
Vast and more expansive than the universe She formed with
Her hands,
I cannot comprehend it.

For ages, men, mostly men, have tried to define Her,
They have attempted to colonize Her Spirit.
They have fought battles and wars just to figure Her out,
And have tried to box Her in and restrict Her movement for
their own peace of mind.
They thought that if they could accurately take hold of her,
They could escape the prisons of their own making.

Believe me, I get it!
We want to get it right on this side of glory because what
comes after feels much more overwhelming than mysterious.
Few have crossed over to the other side and returned to the
land of the living
So we could know the way.
We want to be sure,
Before we take that last breath.
We want to know,
And will spend a lifetime obsessing over the unknown
hoping that all of our worrying will set us free.

But our obsession only drives us further into captivity,
And pushes us to the very brinks of insanity!

Who can know the mind of this God?
Who can control the one who put the foundations of the
earth into its place?
Who can advise the one who strung the stars in the sky,
Holding them up with merely a breath so that they don't
collapse into the sun?

Who can adequately pontificate on this God?
The arrogance of it!

Is God really asking us to have the right beliefs about such
deep mysteries we have not even begun to understand?
Is the accuracy of our beliefs what determines faithfulness?
Righteousness? Salvation?
Whatever happened to justice, love, and humility, virtues
that far too often get sacrificed on the altar of orthodoxy?
Maybe God isn't asking us to have all the right answers but to
have faith enough that She is leading and guiding us the
entire way.
So that even though we walk through literal, physical hell
and back, God remains
Holding and keeping us
Protecting us
Fiercely fighting on behalf of us
Just like any mother would

So I will fear no evil
For God is with me
I will not fear the man wagging his finger, threatening me
with hellfire if I don't fall in line
I will not fear the decrees of the empires, who pretend to
speak for God only so they can oppress the people of God
I will not fear their empty words
I will not fear the examples they have made of those who
resisted

I refuse to be governed by fear of what I cannot know
I will live radically by faith
Faith in the risen Christ
Who I am convinced died so that we all could live
And I know that God's table is big enough for all of us
And that God's house has room for all of us
And that God's goodness and mercy is so great that it covers
all of us and can keep us all from falling

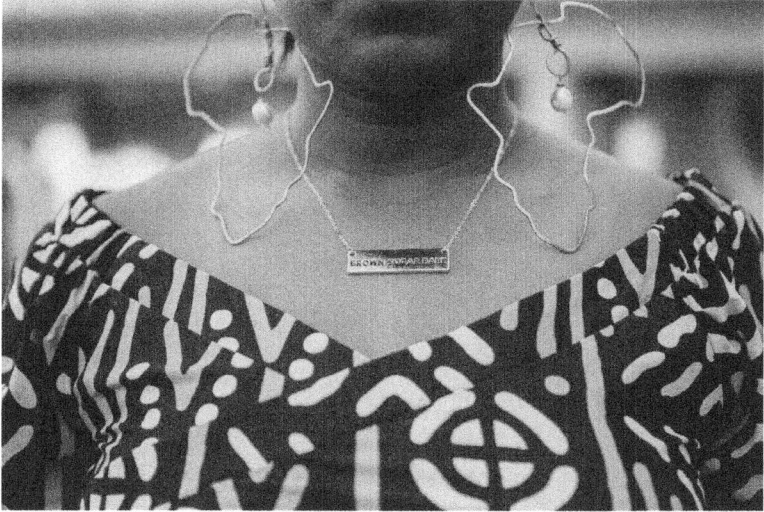

Chapter 7: What I Am Not Going to Do

Confession: I have overextended myself for people in my life who were unable to reciprocate with love and kindness. Because of my own history of neglect and trauma, at times I have allowed people to walk all over me instead of setting firm boundaries of what I will and will not tolerate. In many instances I have called it grace, wanting to be gracious to those who appeared to be struggling more than I. But it wasn't grace at all.

As I reflect on how I got here, I see that this behavior stems from historical and familial patterns, specific instances where I was called on to attend to the emotional needs of others at the expense of my own. I can name countless ways in which experiences from my childhood (and quite honestly even in adulthood) reinforced the belief that to belong, I needed to show up in this way. And so, I did.

Even as I write this, the overwhelming drive to protect others' identities makes me feel as if I cannot be as transparent and vocal with my own story. But I am willing to take a step of faith and vulnerability here because my story is commonplace for so many Black women. After leaving an institution where I worked for years, I felt privately ashamed for wanting to speak honestly about my experiences. The need to protect a space where I felt harmed kept me from being more candid about why I needed to leave, out of fear of being punished and marginalized more than I already was. Instead of being honest, I opted to pacify those who held power over me, offering comfort and grace (that word again), when I should have called people out. It felt safer that way. I am convinced that bottling up my pain, instead of naming it where it needed to be named, not only prolonged the healing process but made it difficult for me to form new, healthy relationships in other places.

This is only one example of where I have put the needs of others before my own; I could write whole books about so many more. But I am not as concerned about telling all the ways in which this has happened as I am about shaking free of the pattern that has caused me to protect others more than I protect myself.

The work that I am doing today to attend to my emotional wellness dropped off somewhere in my early twenties, and I have only picked that work up again in recent years. To be quite honest, I did not really take it seriously until COVID-19 hit because I did not have the time. I was too busy with family, putting out fires at work, pursuing a PhD, trying hard to maintain a vegan diet (it's work, y'all), balancing finances, serving on a board, starting a nonprofit, keeping up with my writing, and all the other things that Black women do.

Right before COVID-19 grasped hold of our community, I started a new journal. On the first page, I articulated how frustrated I was with how things were going in my life. It felt like doors of opportunity kept closing in my face and I couldn't shake this deep anguish in my heart that had been building over the previous few months. On the second page of the journal, I listed four things that I wanted to focus on over the next few months. It was the start of Lent and I felt like I needed to lean into the season in a way that I hadn't before. With intentionality, I declared that I needed to focus on healthy relationships, direction, Divine favor, and wellness at all levels.

At the time, I did not know how prophetic these words would be, as over the last few months these have become the areas that define my life. COVID-19 forced me into community with myself first and foremost, giving me the space to evaluate what was important without running a hundred miles an hour. And it hurt like hell. In addition, it forced a program that I intended to host in-person online.

Relationships with close friends that I thought were solid broke apart, revealing to me things that I knew but wanted to ignore. Dynamics within my larger family system resurfaced with the passing of my grandmother, making me feel as insecure and vulnerable as I felt when I was thirteen years old.

The murder of George Floyd at the hands of the City of Minneapolis police, the same institution I work for, intensified all of the pain and trauma I was already experiencing. The cumulative nature of all of these things, while also trying to finish out the second year of my PhD program and homeschooling my two kids, made me feel as if I had reached the end of my proverbial rope and had absolutely nothing left to hang on to.

I felt at my wit's end. And at the same time, I remembered the words that I wrote in that journal several months before all these things transpired. Relationships. Direction. Favor. Wellness. Wellness. Wellness. I was already in therapy and had found a Black woman therapist (thank you Jesus) right before COVID-19 hit. I was in a healthy environment within an African Methodist Episcopal congregation, which not only consisted of Sunday service but a dynamic group of women meeting together on Monday evenings for fellowship and prayer. And I was exercising. And staying on top of my dietary restrictions. And getting outside. And writing. And praying. And doing as much as I could to be well, not just in order to survive, but to thrive. Period.

This chapter reflects my inner struggle, and more accurately, the struggle in establishing and maintaining healthy boundaries in relationships. Although all the chapters I have written in this book reflect work in progress, this chapter does this the most. The process is simultaneously liberating and frustrating but it is work that I must take on regardless if I do not want to continue the same patterns that have plagued my family, and quite frankly our people, for generations.

I write these words, as well as the words that follow, because I have heard it said that we are only as sick as our secrets. Many of us were raised with the belief that in order to protect others, and inevitably ourselves, that we need to keep things to ourselves—no matter how much they hurt. But as I look at close and distant relationships, I can tell you that secrecy doesn't work; it only lessens the possibility for healing and transformation.

Running
I was the person whose hands instantly turned cold and sweaty
And whose heart dropped into the bottom of her chest
And whose head started swirling like a merry-go-round
round and round at the first sign of conflict

I was the person who wanted to run for the mountains
And intensely prayed for the Second Coming
And who retreated internally at the slightest feeling of
tension, animosity or strife

Now I realize there is no need to run
I don't have to run and hide just because the boogie man
appears
Instead I can be like the tree
Firmly planted by rivers of water
Whose leaves may wither from time to time as the seasons
change and the storm rages
But whose roots remain and endure forever

Wishes
I just want you to be well
I just want you to be
I just want you to
I just want you
I just want
I just
I

Resolutions
I will not cry on the job
I will not cry on the job
I will not cry on the job
I will not cry on the job

Running Revisited
I am not running away from my problems,
Instead I am confronting them, knowing I have the agency to
walk away.
I don't have to put up with abuse, deceit, or anything that
calls into question what I already know to be true about
myself.

I have options
I have a future
My destiny lies in embracing it, not insisting that I face all the
demons thrown my way
After all, demons don't get saved
There is no delivering them

Our best option is to develop a powerful defense, cast them out, and move on, not stay and fight until we are battered and bruised and unable to move

I'm moving now, while I have all of my wits about me
And that's not running
It's freedom

Interruption
Surrounded by a team of peers, there she sat completely frustrated because of how they continued to interrupt her as she spoke—during the five minutes she was allotted to speak, nonetheless

First, they offered unsolicited advice,
Magnifying her problems while deflecting their own.
Then there was significant whitesplaining disguised as efforts to ensure her speech was clear when she had barely uttered a word.

She kept trying to gain control of her space and get through all the things she needed to provide information on. But on and on the charade continued. And on and on her heart grew agitated. Reaching her breaking point, she quickly sorted out a few options in her head:

1. Get up and leave
2. Break down in tears
3. Cuss 'em all out
4. Some combination of the first few options

Instead, she chose a new option. Calmly as she could, she issued a cease and desist order. And as soon as she drew attention to the ridiculousness of the situation, it stopped. She had been heard. And being heard felt liberating, even as it felt disorienting to have to come up out of herself to make her case known. Frustrated, she could never fully regain her composure and left as soon as she was able.

Applications Not Being Accepted

I have a mother and a father,
They are both living and well.
They may not be perfect,
But they are mine.

This notice is not to romanticize them,
Or to draw attention to their strengths,
Or glorify their weaknesses,
But to put the world on notice that applications have not or
will ever be open for their positions

Sincerely,

Management

Becky

She fixed her mouth to say that Black women were bitter and
angry,
And that it was because of our anger that we didn't have a
chance in hell of getting a Black man.

She said that with her long blond hair,
And mocha-colored babies,
Holding onto her Black man as if she had won a trophy off
the auction block.

I wanted to rip out her blessed throat so that she would
never be able to repeat those awful words again. I hope I
sound bitter and angry enough for you now

Hoops and Grease

I am working very hard at keeping my issues in check,
To guard against things showing up in places they ought not
to be
In ways they ought not to be
Directed towards people who trigger rather than initiate it in
the first place
But the way your trauma confronts mine

Makes me want to lash out and scream
Come up out of my skin
Take off my hoops
And grease up my face

I know that's not very Christian of me
Which is why I work out this salvation thing day by day
Keep blowing up at me like you do
And we gonna find ourselves working it out together
As philosopher Tobe Nwigwe once said,
"Try Jesus, not me."

People Pleasing
I need not be liked by everyone to know I am deeply loved
I need not go out of my way and break my back
or stress myself out and drive myself insane to win your
approval

I am already approved
I will stop living as if your blessing could make a difference in
my life
And stop acting as if your words have the capacity to make or
break me

Whether you ride with me or not
I will do great things
I will reach my dreams
I will fulfill God's purpose
And I will keep speaking these words over myself until I
believe them way down in my soul

On Love
I must keep reminding myself that I am truly and deeply
loved,
Not because of what I can offer others,
But because of who I am inside.

And that can be hard to remember sometimes,
Because those who love don't always act loving.

In such instances, it has very little to do with me, but their need to feel the same thing I pursue—love.

Every day, we all go around looking for someone to love and affirm us. This doesn't make us weak or needy, this is core to who we are as human beings. However, if we are looking, we are not doing the business of loving or affirming. In our limited capacity, we look without necessarily giving it the best way we can. This is so because so many of us are running on empty and don't know how to give what we lack.

But when the scream, the note, the ominous Facebook post comes, we all stop to extend what we should have been giving in the first place. And sometimes, it's too late. And if it is not too late, we go back to business as usual until someone else cries out for help.

So, here is a gentle reminder for me and for you: love and affirm others relentlessly and unselfishly. And if we all work on being more loving, we will all feel the same love extending back towards us.

And then we will stop searching for it. For we will have it. And we will be whole. And we will be healed.

Agency
In the words of some wise sage,
I don't have to do nothing but stay Black, pay taxes, and die.
And if that is the case,
I have far more agency than the systems tells me I have.

If I don't like the choices before me,
I can imagine and create my own.
After all, I am modeled in the image of my Creator who spoke into existence whole worlds out of nothingness.

I may not be able to string together galaxies and solar systems,
Or create new species of animals from mere fragments in the

ground.
But I can take that racist sexism you pass off as truth and
create new opportunities for myself and others that don't
revolve around our oppression.

Options, baby, options.
I need not submit myself to these confining institutions to
survive.

Acknowledgment
I know you are hurting immensely
I can't imagine all the pain and suffering that you are going
through
I can offer you my best thoughts, love, and perhaps a hug
during this difficult time
But I won't offer you my heart to beat up on to make yourself
feel better
That's not support, it's abuse

Reminder II
Dearest Ebony,

Please remember to put down the burden that others made
you carry in response to their own pain. It was never yours
to bear the folly of human beings.

Stop wearing the pain as a badge of honor,
Like an important tidbit that has to find itself in every
conversation, dearest one.
Remember that you are free now,
Leave that cross buried at Golgotha and come up out of those
grave clothes.
They do nothing for you but make you look dead.

Honesty
I want to pick up the phone to tell you how bogus you are,
But you are blocking my calls.

So rather than vocalize my frustration,

My resentment,
And my loneliness,
I have to find a way to be well without you,
And without ever telling you just how much your behavior
has affected me.

So, I pray.
I read.
I write.
I walk.
I talk long baths.
I see a therapist.
I am mindful about what I eat (most days).
I do all of these things in attempt to repair my heart.
But the aching never goes away,
And the hurt feels so deep.

Living with the fact that I will never be vindicated,
And may never get closure,
Hurts like hell.
I can't shake that no matter how much I try!
This is a hurt that the passage of time won't heal,
So I guess I will have to learn to forgive and release you so
that bitterness and resentment doesn't set in my heart.

Though I hope you find freedom, forgiveness has nothing to
do with you,
It has everything to do with me and my well-being.
In time, I will get there, but I am not there yet,
So for now, I am focusing on moving through it and accepting
life without you in it.
For the sake of my sanity.
For the sake of my family.
For the sake of my future.

Voices
Fear is a beast,
Slowly and surely it destroys.

It kills your confidence,
Strips your pride,
And makes you question everything you know to be true
about who you are and whose you are–
All because the people inside yourself said you should.

But if you pay attention to the voices long enough,
You will recognize they sound more like that one relative
who never believed in you,
The teacher who never gave you a chance,
The minister who said you weren't enough,
The friend who never really was your friend anyway.

Those people are no longer there,
But their voices remain.
You've internalized them and given them power over your
life!
Time to send out eviction notices and get the naysayers
inside of your head out,
Because you already have everything you need.

Today you possess the knowledge, skill, and wherewithal to
address the challenges you face,
Today you possess the expertise to apply for that job, start
that business, write that book, run for that open
Congressional seat!
You just don't believe it because the negative voices are
drowning your wisdom out.
Your thinking will become clearer and your confidence will
become surer once they leave.

Aquarius Behavior
I don't want to be that girl who has nothing to say when you
greet me,
But after hello and how are you, my mind draws a blank and I
fumble around for words to speak that sound intelligent and
if not, at least interesting.

My hope is that I ask intriguing questions and respond in attentive ways but half the time, I have left the conversation and am focused on the color of your sweater, your banging earrings, or your flawless smile.

Or the next book I want to write.

So, don't be surprised if you ask me how my day is going and I respond, "my favorite color is blue" or if you tell me about what you do, and I look confused. In my mind, I think you said you are a teacher but maybe you are a banker or a musician, I am not sure at this point.

Sorry!

I got caught up in my imagination, something you said sent me on a journey into my own thoughts. Now I am thinking about whole worlds I can create all because you said you like to dance, I think. I promise, it has nothing to do with you, you seem wonderful after all! It's just me being a whole lot of me, the awesome, awkward me.

Welcome Back
I am coming back to myself
Starting to feel human again
Less awkward and disengaged
I can manage a conversation without checking out because I am afraid

She Who Is With Us
They laugh and mock us as we cry out to God for relief,
They rejoice with gladness as they spill our blood in the streets,
And they smile as they cut programs that help the poor

Their bellies are full as they hoard resources that should go to treating cancer, putting kids through college, and ensuring that the social safety net is broad enough, lest anyone of us should fall (because we will).

They are smug in their disdain for life. So, they poison the waters, burn through the ozone and destroy the good earth that God has made for their own selfish gain.

And yet, they continue to hold out hope that God won't care. That God will look the other way as they crush the face of the dispossessed into the earth. That's why they pray and tithe and fast and hold onto "conservative" beliefs, hoping against hope that God will forgive them of the evil that they release upon the earth.

Today they smile,
And laugh,
And mock,
And rejoice at what their hands have done.

Little do they know that God is here,
That God is here to save and deliver those who are crushed by oppression from the hands of their enemies.
Little do they know that the Messiah is here, to restore balance upon the earth, to redeem everything and everyone that has suffered under the hand of tyranny.

Little do they know that the jig is up. They will be called to give an account for every evil deed:

For every Black boy they murdered in cold blood,
For every acre of land they stole from the Americas to South Africa,
For every woman they denied access to birth control,
For every morsel of good they withheld from the mouth of a two-year-old child (even though they are pro-life),
For every person with disease they denied access to care,
For every immigrant and refugee they deported, even though they destroyed their homelands,
For every man they refused to prosecute for rape,
For every human being they falsely incriminated,
For every person they maligned on account of their race, religion, gender, sexual orientation, or ability,

For every person they denied the opportunity to be fully human, fully loved and embraced as image bearers of the living God,
For every time they followed evil instead of good.

They silence us because our existence bears witness against them. What they don't know is that even in death our blood testifies against them. And God hears, just as She has always heard. And God will restore us. God will bring salvation to the poor and the needy. God has remembered every single person this system has forgotten and will bring us refuge this day.

Ode to the Spirit
The Spirit left at nine o'clock.
She walked me to the door and begged me not to leave her,
But there was no place for her inside.
They would kill her inside.

"I will be back at 5 p.m.,
Then we will walk and play,
I will take you to the lake and we can run around.
We'll eat and stay up way beyond our bedtime,
Laughing on the couch until we fall asleep."

"Ok," she obliged,
And I went in.
I rushed through the day a lesser version of myself,
But I survived.

I met the Spirit at the door at 5 p.m.,
Hand in hand we walked to the car.
We played with the children once they got out of school.
Walked to the lake after they rested to write and just be.
We ate dinner with the family.
Talked and laughed on the couch when we should have been sleeping,
Knowing that in the morning we would start the same routine again.

On and on it went like this for days.
Days turned into weeks,
Weeks into months,
Months into years of leaving the Spirit at the beginning of the
day and returning to her in the evening.

But after a while, I stopped looking for her to greet me.
In attempt to make it through, I ignored the Spirit,
And in the Spirit's absence, there were no more walks,
No more play with the children,
No more times at the lake pouring through journals.

There were no more late-night conversations 'til one in the
morning, laughing and crying over the troubles of the day.
In an attempt to survive, I gave up me.
I gave up my life.
I stopped breathing.
I stopped creating.
I stopped being.

Then one day,
I hit a wall.
The barrier that I had built for years between myself and the
Spirit broke away piece by piece by piece like fragile paint
chips.
I screamed into the earth as the oppression I allowed myself
to endure for years fell off,
Piercing me as it was ripped from my body,
Threatening to destroy me if I didn't yield.

But the Spirit held me as the yoke of oppression fell into that
Great Sea,
You see, the Spirit was in control!
She who I insisted remain on the outside,
Who I stopped returning to at the end of the day,
Who I stopped walking with,
Playing with,

Talking to,
And laughing with up into the wee hours of the morning.

This Spirit had found a way inside,
And was coming to rescue me from the shell I had become!
From that day, I vowed to never leave the Spirit behind,
I would not abandon her.
I would love her fiercely.
I would refuse to cut off pieces of me just to make it through
the day.
No, the Spirit was the only way I could survive the hellish
ordeal that awaited me like clockwork between 9–5 every
day.

Adedayo

Chapter 8: Black Joy

Joy is an action word. While many people attribute it to a feeling, it is more than an articulation of how we feel on any given day. Every day we make a conscious decision to access joy. The situations surrounding us might suggest that we have very little to be joyful about—lost employment, foreclosure, disease, toxic relationships, ongoing police violence, the fact that #45 still occupies the White House. But it is in these moments when joy is the most critical.

This is what so many gospel artists attest to in their songs about joy. Be it Ron Kenoly, the Colorado Mass Choir, Kirk Franklin, Yolanda Adams, just to name a few—for these artists, joy is about having something that is otherworldly, something that cannot be taken away by the devil or anyone else. It is a state of mind that is contrary to one's own circumstances.

Joy is also an act of intentional resistance in a society that does not want us to exist. For over four hundred years, this country has tried to subdue, silence, and extinguish us simply for breathing. Yet, despite what they have done to us, they have not had unbridled access to our spirits. They could not and cannot kill our will. This is because for over four hundred years, we have created spaces and opportunities to exercise joy and to speak that joy over others around us. For over four hundred years, we as a people have declared that come hell or high water, this system cannot police our joy.

Joy comes forth in our exuberant and expressive preaching, teaching, and expository oratory skills. It is evidenced in our works of art. It is visible in the way that we dress and the way that we do our hair. And in the way we dance, from the ring shout that our ancestors practiced to the twerking some of us do today; the vigor in which we move, as if we are

trampling demons beneath our feet, is evidenced in our
sweat-out hair.

And joy is evidenced through our song—the songs that we
sing to one another and to ourselves. You can feel it in a
worship service, at a concert, or in a small gathering of folks
as one breaks out in song to encourage others. There is
power in the collective energy that gets passed from person
to person as we catch the spirit being conjured up in
moments like these.

Joy is that sense of nostalgia shared among us when a song
comes on the radio that takes us back to our much younger
selves. We recall who we were and who we were with the
first time we heard Fresh Prince and Jazzy Jeff's
"Summertime" or Arrested Development's "Tennessee" (I
was in elementary school when both songs came out and my
family still lived on 37th and Lisbon in Milwaukee. Every
time I hear "Summertime," my mind flashes back to those
days). Or how we felt when Tevin Campbell romanced
Tatyana Ali's character on *Fresh Prince of Bel Air* (I was
jealous because I had a huge crush on him back then). We
hold these memories sacred. At least I do!

And joy is felt in the way that we gather together. Barbeques.
House parties. Block parties. Summer festivals. Family
reunions. Sunday dinners. Joy is shared when we are in each
other's presence and we can sit with each other without an
agenda and without pretense, to just be. This is only one of
the devastating consequences of COVID-19, as it has robbed
many of us of the opportunity to honor these rituals of
coming together.

Because joy is so important, we must protect and recreate it,
not only to survive, but to thrive. This system doesn't want
that for us! This system would rather have us angry and
beside ourselves because of the cumulative trauma we
endure. They would rather that we fall apart and explode on
those around us just to get some relief. They do not want us

to access joy. They do not want us to tap into the reservoir of faith and endurance that has gotten our people through all these years. They do not want us to sing and dance like we are doing battle against the very gates of hell. And this is all the more reason why we must practice it as if our very lives depended on it. Because they do. This is what the collection of poems in this chapter are all about.

Wings

Carefree little Black girl, I see you with your arms flapping around like wings on a bird that is unbound and unbothered.
Your good church dress is covered in dust,
And you have sweated out all that beautiful, black hair,
That your mamma took all night to hot comb and plait into perfect rows.

She's gonna be so mad,
And she just might holler,
But you're too busy running around with the neighborhood kids to seem to mind what your dear mamma thinks.

So be free, carefree little Black girl
And do you

Very Good

I thank you God, for I am fearfully and wonderfully made,
You knew my unformed body and declared every part of me good.
My kinky, curly hair.
My dark brown skin that glows.
My eyes, lips, nose, and toes.
You said that all of me was very good.

My narrow hips.
My petite frame.
The way I smile.
How I laugh.
You said all of me was very good.

And now that I've birthed and nursed two children,
And am just a tad bit older,
And cellulite laces the tops of my thighs,
And stretch marks across my waist are unrelenting,
And that c-section line pangs me just a bit from time to time,
And the grays are starting to crowd my crown,
And I can't wear the things I used to without being in some
serious adult pain,
I bet you still think I'm pretty fly–
And find me very good.

Thank You
He told me that he liked my smile,
I didn't deflect.
I just said thank you.
Progress. One thank you at a time.

Rich
My pockets aren't very deep,
And my bank account isn't very full.
My savings are minuscule,
And sometimes I have more month than my income will pay
for.

But I am rich,
Full of goodness,
Overflowing in love,
Surrounded by loved ones who light up my day,
Clothed in the Spirit who continuously prompts me to pray,
I thank God for the wealth that can't be measured by this
world.
And for that reason, it can't be stolen either.

For I embody the history, the music, the wisdom, the
spirituality, and the way of knowing of my ancestors.
It is generations deep.
Yes, it can be found on the shores of America,
But it was birthed deep in the soil of Mother Africa.
The same soil God used to shape Adam and Eve is where my

wealth lies.
Now that is true riches!
I can't take any of this to the bank,
But it sure does sustain me more than any dollar can.

Glory to Glory
Gradually I am finding the healing my soul and spirit needs
Healing the pain of deep memories
By writing a new narrative
Shedding the lies and deceit
In pursuit of the truth

Diva
She walked up in the spot
Rocking 3" blue stilettos
Ebony-colored hair freshly twisted
Shining so brightly, the sun must have kissed it
Dark brown skin wrapped in shea butter cream scented with
lavender and eucalyptus
Wearing hoops as big as the moon
And lip gloss the color of maroon

Her dress coordinated with her shoes—and of course was
blue–
A different shade but blue all the same
Her favorite
And for good reason, it looked good on her

In one hand, she carried her morning coffee
Black—no sugar, no cream
In the other, a story I am sure
About how she got here
Who her people are
Why she dances so freely
And how she loves so fiercely

Chocolate covered diva,
Go ahead and do what you do

Transform the world
With your heart and your style

90s
Banana Now & Laters
Tupac and Biggie Wars
Crooklyn and Selena
Nancy Kerrigan and OJ
Black president
Fresh
Fly
Baggie Jeans
Dookie Braids
Kris Kross
Ayesha
Jodeci Boots
Rodney King, riots, and attempts at getting along
Dodging bullets
Avoiding the dealers next door and the man down the street
walking around with a piece
Feelings of fear mixed with euphoria
Like summertime
For Us By Us
And it truly was us until it wasn't
Too weak
On bended knee
First love and first heartbreak
Sacred Fridays and
Lazy Saturday mornings
Oh the 90s
You were special to me

This is Me (Love All of Me)
I,
Black,
Woman.
Strong, sufficient, reliable,
Trusting, to a fault perhaps.

Reserved, only because I suck at small talk (One can only ask how you are doing so many times in a conversation before it gets weird and goes south).
Passionate, sometimes aloof, only because I am thinking about the worlds I am creating in my mind where we all get to be free.
It's usually not because I find you uninteresting.
Usually.

Lover of the written word, how they twist and twirl on a page like the coils on my head, wrapping tightly around each other 'til they form a coherent whole.

Meaning-making, theories and dissertations—my happy place, full of wonder and awe. Enveloped by neo-soul, gospel, jazz, and R&B in the background—take your pick, it's all wonderful to me. One voice, one sound, one soul belting out melodies, helping us reconcile this existence over the last four hundred years with who we should have been. Where we should have been.

Unapologetically Christian!
Saved, sanctified, Holy Ghost filled, water-baptized,
Jesus on my mind, only some of the time

African, conscious, woke,
Pork-abstaining, my daddy taught me that,
Grits avoiding, they will never touch these lips!
Can't play spades to save my life
And after all these years still can't seem to figure double-dutch out.

This is me.
This all of me.
All 5'4"
170 pounds.
Vegan and gluten free.
All of Me.

Love all of me.
Both my curves and my curls.
Both my Blackness and my faith.
Both my femininity and my sensuality.
Love all of me.

A Song of Praise to Black Women
I see you
How the world keeps trying to pull you down
How people insist on putting you in your place for speaking
too loudly
Giving your opinion so freely
Loving others so fiercely.

They'd much rather you keep silent
Stay hidden
Play small
Because then you become their equals
They do it because your smile is just too bright for their
sensitive eyes
And your arms too strong for their weak bodies.

And your love?
A love that moves mountains,
Raises the dead,
Heals the sick,
And feeds the hungry?
Far too great for their tepid attempts at affection!

Black woman!
She who is created in the image of God
Whose face reflects the shining sun
Whose lips creates
Whose words heal, set free, and redeem!

Black women!
So powerful and so free
Pay no attention to your enemies
Those who seek to steal, kill, and destroy your spirit

Those who will throw shade at everything you do
Not because you did anything wrong, but because they envy
you.

Shine so brightly
Stand up tall
Love without repentance
Hair shrinkage and all.

Shine beauty shine
Let your inner glow shake the earth's foundations
Let your spirit make hell tremble.

Sister, do you
Paint your lips
Adorn your ears—the bigger, the better
Rock the heels—or flats—or go barefoot if you must.

Just do you!
And do it all!
Relentlessly.

Black Men
I saw you on TV
And I smiled because you were there
So much Black brilliance
Such sheer black joy
Unapologetically lighting up the airwaves with your space
and your grace
Your existence makes this life worth living

Brothas
What can I say with the words at my disposal to describe you
To me, you are the exemplary expression of beauty,
brilliance, and excellence
Clearly superior
Clearly poised and positioned to take on the challenges of the
world without missing a beat

Brothas
Tall and dark like ebony
Short and cream like a peach
I love you all
The way you shine
The way you take up space
Your style
Your swag
Your cologne
Your humor
Your intellect
Cuts through the layers of crap this world keep trying to pass
off as normal

No wonder they keep trying to cut you down
In you lies the power to change systems and outcomes for
the good

Brothas,
Keep shining
Keep loving and embracing
Keep deconstructing, keep resisting, keep building
Keep bringing us into new spaces
No matter what the dissenters say

Seven
Yes the world is burning
But I am going to celebrate you with all that I have within me
Because you deserve to be a carefree Black boy
To jump, to dance, to run around as fast as you can. You
deserve that every day but especially today. Today is your
day and I want you to be you.

Holy Ghost
I get it now
Why the church mothers used to dance so hard
And the fathers kept up with that one-two step
And the elders fell out in the Holy Ghost

Religiously
Like Sunday dinners

You have to keep dancing
To keep from going crazy
You have to keep shouting
To keep the devil from taking over
You have to get slain in the Holy Ghost
To keep your body grounded in the reality that this is not all
there is

There is more
On the other side of Jordan
Through the Red Sea
Beyond the blazing fire and soul-sucking desert that is this
life

Let me go get my good shoes, I will dance 'til we get there

Conclusion: Not a Destination, a Journey

I started 2017 mad as hell! Like many people, I was upset about the 2016 presidential election and feared the worst for Black folks. Unsure of where our country was headed, or at least convinced that it was headed straight to hell like Dr. King said, I questioned the purpose of my new job with the City of Minneapolis looking at how stress and trauma show up in the community.

Not a week after the new guy took office, I was in Maryland for a work-related conference. Away from home, I cried out to God for clarity. I felt as if pure evil surrounded me and I wanted nothing more than to leave and go somewhere comfortable. Like Canada. That way I wouldn't have to deal with what was going on in the Oval Office and I could ignore the problems that were surfacing in my own life.

The truth was, even before #45 was elected, even before he announced his candidacy, I was struggling. After spending years in the academy and lay pastoral, I grew tired of trying to justify my experience in spaces that were not designed for people like me. No matter how sanctified I was, how well I preached, which faith-based so-called progressive space I was a part of, I kept hitting my head against the proverbial glass ceiling. I was told that my interpretation of marginalized folks like the Prophet Amos was not scholarly. And that my approach to Old Testament favorites like Cain and Abel lacked a certain nuance that was commonplace in white, liberal congregations. And that my desire to talk about the multicultural church experience was cute but not my place because I was not a part of that movement. These were all white spaces, and all led by white men, who were only interested in my voice so long as I validated what they already believed, not if I challenged them based on my particularity as a dark skinned Black woman.

Despite my struggle, I assumed that participation in these spaces was the only way to be. I believed that God had called me to the ministry of reconciliation and that I had to fulfill that call regardless of what it did to my mental and spiritual health. And so I persisted, continued despite the hurt. But I was growing tired of trying to justify my personhood to those who only wished to use me as a prop to further their own agenda and who had no real intention of embracing me.

Outside of my role in the church, which was all voluntary, I worked in other arenas. To get through college, I worked in retail and banking. I was even a licensed insurance agent for a while. It feels like that era of my life was forever ago! Halfway through seminary, I started working in a nonprofit and felt like I had found a place outside of formal church ministry that I could give my heart to. From 2009–2011, I worked for a national organization that focused on hunger and poverty relief. Then in 2011, I started working for a local nonprofit where I stayed for nearly six years. And it was a good six years. In that time frame, I felt like I found myself and honed my voice as a writer and as a minister, even though the job had nothing to do with ministry. It was just that the racial justice work resonated with me so deeply it influenced how I interpreted the biblical text. My theological framework was shaped by the experience of working in these environments more than all the years I had spent in church and Christian Higher Education combined.

I transitioned from this place that really nurtured my development to another in 2016. With this transition, I was afforded the opportunity to think about my personal journey, particularly regarding healing and spirituality differently. I took part in a fellowship with mostly women of color, where I was encouraged to practice intentional self-care. This language went against everything I knew about being a Black woman, namely being the sacrificial martyr willing to take on the burdens of the world to save the world. It was this line of thinking that kept me in spaces that did not serve me for far too long! Yet, as I practiced self-care, I saw areas in myself that needed to heal. So I began to journal in a way that I had not before. I poured through pages and pages, reflecting on who I was, who I was not, and who I wanted to be. More than anything, I no longer wanted to be the one who tried to fit in. I was no longer comfortable, if I ever really was, in working to gain the approval of others. When I came to that realization, I understood that more possibilities existed for me as a Black Christian woman to lead from my convictions and values; I would just have to create them.

This book is one of many results of this realization; the Kinky Curly Theological Collective is one of the others. The Kinky Curly Theological Collective was born out of a desire to create a space where I could exist and be wholly and completely me. I wanted a space where I could completely and unapologetically stand in who I was as a dark skinned woman of the African diaspora. I would not have to choose between my heritage, my skin color, or my femininity; I could be all three along with all my other intersecting identities. And I could stand unapologetically in my faith, not shrinking back to make others feel comfortable with my expression of faith. And I could center my experiences, my expertise, and my education, convinced that what I possessed was enough to do God's work in the world. I didn't need to prove anything. I just needed to be.

I created the Kinky Curly Theological Collective to give me a space to be and to also grant this space to other women of the African diaspora. I was intentional about including not only African American women but African immigrants, believing that our healing as a people are tied together. As I turned this idea around in my spirit, using my kitchen walls as a makeshift canvas to map out ideas with sticky notes, I knew that we would focus on healing, spiritual and theological reflection, and would also nurture our own practice around theological development. The latter was important to me because I was not seeing our experiences and particularities as central points of theological consideration. Even in so-called progressive spaces, our identities as African women of the diaspora were marginal, considered divergent to the otherwise "normal" Christian faith experiences. I wanted to flip that notion upside down, understanding that the biblical text is comprised of example after example of those who have been marginalized against "normal" imperial structures of their day.

One thing I wrestled with early on was whether this would be an explicitly Christian space. I struggled with this because I knew of women in my circle who had been deeply hurt by the church as a result of racism, sexism, homophobia, respectability politics, and obsession with the prosperity gospel to the exclusion of the pure gospel of the Black Palestinian Jesus who was just as marginalized and exploited as the rest of us. And I held this tension, even within my own body, about how I could continue to follow a faith that had been used by whites to justify the theft of American Indian lands, the genocide of native bodies, the enslavement of Black bodies, and the pillaging of Black women's bodies. I wondered how I could make sense of the dichotomy if I was serious about Black liberation? The more and more I listened to myself and listened to the groans of others around me, the more I felt compelled to broaden the space from being Christian to those who practiced spirituality, whether that spirituality had Christian roots or not.

For me, the shift in the space had to be as inclusive as possible. I did not want to be a part of anything where I felt I couldn't be my whole self or had to limit pieces of myself to be accepted. I didn't want that for myself and I also did not want it for any woman who would be a part of this collective. I wanted and yearned for liberation, which meant that I couldn't create any systems of oppression in this theological space, even if it was with my Black face.

In deciding to expand the space I, by extension, ended up expanding my theology. I did not anticipate this evolution but felt completely led and supported by the Holy Spirit as I did. Honestly, it felt unnerving because for the first time in my Christian experience, I was questioning concepts that I had always held as fundamental truths. But the idea of truth and who gets to define the truth had to be examined, especially in our societal context where people in power are redefining truth with alternative facts. This is not unique to our time and place; truth has always been a tool of the empire to impose certain laws and control behavior. In looking at different cultural and spiritual expressions, I also wondered how multiple, intersecting truths can make up something that we cannot entirely see right now, but see in time as the full picture of God's truth is revealed. These things affirmed for me that God's truth is found in every culture, every place, in every corner of the world. Cone (1997) says it well in his book *God of the Oppressed,*

> *"The Divine is more than what we think, perceive, and dream at any moment in time and it is this 'more' or otherness in divine reality that makes it necessary for theology to recognize its conceptual limitations. Divine revelation, about which theology speaks, cannot be boxed into linguistic formulations derived from human experience. Any theology that fails to accept the finitude of its categories, speaking as if it knows the whole truth and nothing but the truth, is guilty of blasphemy, that is, of an ideological distortion of divine reality (p. 87)."*

Despite the limitations of theology, we know that our experiences are valid. My experience as a woman of the African diaspora in the church is valid. The fact that Jesus came and rescued me, showed me His love, and nurtured me into adulthood when I did not always have the love and support I wanted is valid. How the Spirit has shepherded and guided me when I did not always want to be kept, is valid.

And the testimonies of my mother and grandmother and ancestors who held on to this same Jesus to get through slavery, survive Jim Crow, and escape the South, is valid. As Cone likewise affirms, these stories become the truth of our lives. "Jesus is now my story, I don't have to prove it, only bear witness to it (p. 98)."

When I recognize that my truth is connected to my story and my experience, I have more space to recognize that others' truths are connected to their stories and their experiences. I can sit with the stories and experiences of others without feeling that I must prove mine or that they must prove theirs—we just bear witness to our own stories while holding the others. And those whose stories exist only to oppress and exploit others get a chance to see that their truth is a farce; it is not standard or absolute. It is only because of the power they wield that they can claim it is.

So, before I close out the pages of this book, I must ask: what is your truth? I ask this question specifically to Black women because we have ignored our witness for so long that we do not even believe and trust one another let alone ourselves. A couple of months ago, I hosted the second annual conference for the Kinky Curly Theological Collective. In advertising it, another sister completely chastised me, saying that this was a gathering full of Jezebels and would amount to nothing more than us showing how ugly we can look. And then she made gross misstatements about our sexuality, hoping to frighten us into silence. Yes, that seriously happened. Her sentiment may be more on the extreme side, and yet feelings of unworthiness lay at the root of her hurtful words. Because we live in a culture where misogynoir is big business, we have all internalized similar dispositions that we must fight against daily. This book is how I fight. The Kinky Curly Theological Collective is how I fight. The doctoral program that I am currently in is another way that I fight. All these ways, and so many more, give me the opportunity to fight and center the truth of who we truly are as Black women. It is a truth that has the power to transform our lives and turn the world upside down, and for this reason, we can stay silent about it no longer.

This is my truth. And this truth is the Gospel according to a Black Woman.

Once More Before I Go: A Story

Black women. People will try us. They will despise us. They will negate our testimony because it contradicts their version of truth. They will even try to bury the truth we carry in our bones because if we let it out, their pretend worlds will come crumbling down.

They don't silence us because we are worthless. They silence us because we are powerful!

So, we must keep speaking. We must keep preaching and teaching. We must keep telling our stories, and the stories of other Black women, so that the entire world will reckon with the wisdom that they have abandoned.

This is the charge that I leave before us, and it is the charge that I lay before myself, knowing that as long as our voices are silenced, we can never know peace.

Taking on this challenge, I have prepared one last story before we leave these pages. This story has been something I have been turning over in my spirit for the last several years, namely because the biblical account of this story raises so many questions and seems to sanction the oppression of women, children, and queer individuals.

The story in question here is none other than that found in Genesis 19 where God allegedly destroys Sodom and Gomorrah because of homosexuality. In the text, the main protagonist's wife dies because she refuses to leave the city and this same protagonist's daughters have his children to carry on the family name. I grew up taking these interpretations of the text as the Gospel, never picking apart, much less questioning the absence of women's voices to either explain or vindicate themselves. In this retelling of the story, called *Forgetting Sodom*, I center the voices that have been left out, and tell a more comprehensive narrative of the marginalized characters.

My point in the retelling is to raise the questions we have all asked ourselves privately, afraid to bring up in Bible studies or seminary classrooms for fear of being called a heretic. My point is not to challenge the Bible's authority but to insist that in the scribing of this story thousands of years ago, the male writer—undoubtedly influenced by the patriarchal culture in which he lived—left out some key details. In writing the story, I employ the technique of womanist theologians like Weems, Delores Williams, Wil Gafney, Mitzi Smith, and so many others who interpret the biblical text from our position and experience as Black women. In doing so, my aim is to tell a more comprehensive narrative about the decisions Black women make, particularly when we are pushed up against the wall and the choices before us are less than favorable.

Such considerations illustrate the importance of a process that I call revisiting the sacred register, in this case the biblical text. In revisiting the sacred register, we reclaim the presence and experience of women in the text (who are Afro-Asiatic in origin), we redefine female relationships in the context of the Divine, human relationships, and the earth, and we rewrite/renarrate the stories in the text from the lens of our own experiences as women.

Weems (1993) returns to the sacred text in her book *I Asked for Intimacy*, and re-narrates the story of Leah from Genesis in the biblical text. Weems looks at Leah's story through the eyes of Black women who have returned to romantic relationships where they have been taken advantage of or abused, in order to suggest that Black women do not have to subject ourselves to inaccurate interpretations of the biblical text in order to know and receive love. For Weems and other womanist theologians like her, suffering is not redemptive, but instead leaves us trapped in a cycle of codependence where we end up assigning blame in the relationship to someone else instead of taking responsibility for our own shortcomings.

Similarly, Underwood (2016) returns to the sacred text to expose abuse in the Old Testament book of Job which tells of a man who loses all that he has (including his children) and is afflicted with disease. In the story, God allows these hardships to happen to Job in order to prove to the Devil, Satan—the chief antagonist—that no matter what Job faces in life, Job will trust God. Pushing back against most interpretations of the text, however, Underwood shows that Job himself becomes the abused wife "for no reason other than the abusive 'husband' Yahweh (YHWH) possesses the power to abuse (p.166)." This contrasts with other biblical passages where adherents of YHWH experience punishment or Divine retribution because of something that they did. In this instance, however, Job does nothing wrong. In fact, for all intents and purposes Job appears to be the embodiment of perfection. Yet, he suffers to prove God's point, illustrating that domestic violence is likewise unprovoked and without cause, contradicting the notion that the abused must have done something to deserve the retribution.

Revisiting the sacred text to re-narrate and rewrite positions Black women in a different light. Rather than reinforcing the belief that our suffering is Divinely inscribed, it gives us the ability to imagine other possibilities when and if we encounter gaslighting, mistreatment, and abuse in our relationships. This is the purpose of the following story.

Forgetting Sodom
"Good women listen and obey their husbands.
Good women keep their legs closed.
Good women keep their house.
Good women have their children in line.
Good women know how to pray.
Good women don't misbehave. They don't talk back. They
don't ask questions. They stay in their place."

By the time she was five years old, Jia had fully committed
her grandmother's words to memory. Though her
grandmother had never sat down and taught Jia these words,
hearing them roll off her grandmother's tongue again and
again caused Jia to memorize them just as she had
memorized the alphabet. Still, Jia was confused by the words'
meaning. Did keeping her legs closed mean she couldn't play
soccer with her older brother and his friends? She couldn't
quite figure out how she could kick the ball without
separating one leg from the other. So, she stopped playing.
For a week. Soccer was one of the few things that brought Jia
absolute joy, and she was better at it than most of the other
neighborhood children, including her brother. She surmised
that her grandmother had to mean something else regarding
this keeping your legs closed business.

When Jia wasn't playing soccer or reading some book that
her parents had forced under her nose, she spent time with
her two best friends, Ness and Cynthia. Ness, short for
Vanessa, was small like Jia, with curly black hair that her
parents kept cut short and chocolate brown skin that always
smelled like coconut oil. Though all of them were the same
age, Cynthia was much bigger than Jia and Ness. She kept her
wavy brown hair pulled back into a ponytail so it wouldn't
fall into her face and annoy her. Autism. Jia didn't know what
it meant, but she knew that Cynthia had it. The three of them
could be playing marvelously, and suddenly Cynthia would
start yelling or crying for reasons that they did not
understand. When that happened, Jia or Ness would go get

Cynthia's mom, Sanaa, who would drop whatever she was doing to comfort her daughter.

In those days, there were not a lot of jobs outside of the armed forces or teaching. But Cynthia's father, Morris, held on to the barbershop that had been in his family for generations. It was a rarity. Even though times were hard, his clientele held steady as it was one of the last remaining places in the community where Black people could come together and be themselves. Neighborhood organizations and nonprofits were a thing of the past. Churches, mosques, and other faith institutions that wouldn't preach the government's propaganda were raided and shut down with their ministers imprisoned. And state-sanctioned violence was at an all-time high. People were stopped, harassed, and even killed for walking down the street. No one took the risk of being out in public anymore. It was a different world than the one Jia's grandparents had lived in. A world before the Great Incident.

Like most things that made the US look bad, the Great Incident only had a small paragraph in Jia's fifth grade textbook. It followed the fifteen pages of coverage on the Coronavirus of 2020 that killed hundreds of thousands of people around the world in two years. Jia's grandmother told her that elementary schools, including her own in Milwaukee, Wisconsin were shut down for years, sending every child into absolute boredom and driving every parent of every child crazy.

When the Coronavirus finally left, it left not only death in its wake; it also crippled the global economy because no one was buying anything beyond the absolute essentials like hand sanitizer and toilet paper and food. To keep the economy from tanking, the US government provided most families with stimulus checks to encourage them to go out and spend. But people held back the money instead of spending it on the frivolous things that they used to. After all, so many people were unemployed that the government's measly checks did nothing to increase their spending power. Seeing that the stimulus checks did not improve the economy in the way that was hoped (even though it helped people), #45 bullied governors into opening their states back up long before they were ready. This is why the virus lingered so long and claimed so many lives. Because of #45's negligence and general ineptness, the economy did not recover to pre-Coronavirus levels. So the country went to war.

Well, not really the country. But #45. Jia's grandmother, who was usually a very reserved woman, immediately started swearing like a sailor at the mention of #45 or anything that reminded her of #45. The hell that he put the world through, let alone his own country, during his first term in office seemed like a cakewalk compared to his second term. War was a bad idea according to every single economist and political strategist. Even some of the otherwise spineless Republican ones. Like always, he ignored their advice and instigated a conflict with Iran just for the heck of it. Money-hungry a$$ hole.

This is where the details started to fall apart in Jia's memory. Because it wasn't the initial conflict that was the actual Great Incident, but it set the stage for what happened in the thirties and forties. Absolute horror! By 2045, the US was a has-been and was completely done for. Capitalism had progressed from late stage and was finally dead and gone. Its demise claimed more lives than the Coronavirus. Those who could escape the US did so. Others went off the grid to escape the government's prowling eyes as well as the MAGA party who longed for the good ole days and took their hostility out on anyone in their path.

Yet, people couldn't openly talk about the Great Incident. One could easily end up missing if they went beyond the government-sanctioned talking points. But because the neighborhood barbershop was always a safe space, Morris took great liberties in educating the young men who sat in his chair week after week, just as his father had done. He talked about life. Women. Sex. God. The Civil Rights Movement. The Black Lives Matter Movement, including the fierce queer Black women who led the movement. Anything and everything that came to his mind. And anything that the young men asked him about. Even though he was cautioned against being so loose with his lips, his barbershop was the only liberty that he had left, and the only space that Black folks had left to just be. He willingly took the risk and prayed that the government wouldn't catch up with him.

Jia was in the fifth grade when Morris went missing. He left for work one late October morning—the year was 2123—and just never made it in. His wife Sanaa organized a search party for him, but everyone knew what had happened. After about a week of looking for him, they called off the search and accepted the bitter truth for what it was. As much as Morris' disappearance shook Sanaa, it completely disoriented Cynthia—who couldn't understand where her daddy was and why he wouldn't come home to be with her, just as he had done every day since she was born.

Sanaa took her children—Cynthia and her other daughter, Charlene—and moved in with Sanaa's older brother Nakeem who lived across town. They only stayed there for as long as it took Sanaa to get her children's passports and a visa to go to Ghana. Sanaa and Nakeem had an older sibling who had lived there for over twenty years, who had willingly given up their US citizenship. Sanaa knew if she left, she would essentially do the same thing and that there would be no coming back. But she did not care. She did not want herself or her children to end up like Morris, here one day and gone the next. Jia never saw Cynthia again.

As heartbreaking as the whole thing was, Cynthia's family were the lucky ones. A lot of Black folks wanted to emigrate but couldn't for one reason or another. It was only by the grace of God that Sanaa was able to get those passports for her children. Others tried to leave, and it only made their lives worse. Suddenly, there would be a warrant out for the arrest of someone from that household—usually the father, but sometimes an uncle or the oldest child regardless of gender. The warrant was usually baseless, founded on fabricated charges that the arresting officer knew were not true. Proving truth or innocence, however, wasn't the point. Because accessing a lawyer was a luxury reserved only for the rich, someone could easily spend years behind bars before even having their case tried. In desperation, some took plea bargains but doing so cut off the opportunity for them or anyone else in their family getting visas to travel. The times revealed what Black people had always known to be true about their relationship to the US—the government didn't want Black people living in America; and it wasn't content with Black people living anywhere else either.

(2)

The year was 2153 and Jia wasn't a child anymore. Standing 5'8" tall, thin, with waist-length, jet-black locked hair, she now had children of her own who were sixteen and seventeen. She hadn't intended on having her children so close together. As a matter of fact, she had only wanted one, especially after the complicated birth of her firstborn. But her husband Lot wasn't having it. He wanted more. And he had needs, as he always expressed to Jia. Needs that didn't prioritize her own need to heal from the vaginal tear she experienced from pushing out her first. Needs that didn't care that she was still bleeding two months after giving birth. He was the man, so his needs came first.

"Good women listen and obey their husbands . . . Good women don't misbehave. They don't talk back. They don't ask questions. They stay in their place."

After all these years, her grandmother's words still rang loudly in her head. Though Jia didn't really believe them, she didn't like the way Lot got when he was upset. His usual quiet demeanor transformed into something that Jia was not comfortable with. Because of this, Jia tried to keep Lot happy as much as possible, even though she was not happy herself. Her aim was to keep herself and her children safe. And that aim was enough to cause her to yield to Lot's sexual advances even though the very thought of being with him repulsed her.

"You should be glad that I still want you," Lot would often say. *"Don't you know how many other women I could have been with? But I still come home to you."*

Lot wasn't lying. There were plenty of women who wanted him and with whom he could have easily returned the affection. He was tall, dark skinned, full bearded, and built, and looked like Idris Elba looked in 2020. Just fine. The years and the gray had only caused him to be more handsome. He was aging like fine wine. But Jia did not care. In fact, she secretly wished that he would run away with one of those "other women" so her soul and her body could finally be at rest.

Lot was much older than Jia. In fact, he was much older than many people in their small town right outside of Atlanta, called Sodom. Though he was nearing sixty-five, he was a manual laborer during the day, working odd jobs to make a small living for his family. By night, Lot was the community elder, gathering other families into their tiny living room for prayer and devotion. He always seemed to have a word of encouragement for that young couple who were struggling in their marriage, or for the parents whose child had gotten caught up in the system. People loved him for his compassion and willingness to be there for them in their time of need. No one would have suspected the Lot that Jia knew was a completely different person. But two contradictory things can be true at once.

Apparently, God had also fallen for Lot's ruse. Apparently, God could not see into their bedroom at night, and either couldn't see or did not care about the times that Jia had cried herself to sleep after one of their encounters. Maybe Jia was being irrational, but she couldn't keep from thinking like this when things never changed, no matter how much she prayed and fasted. Didn't she also have a connection to God? Didn't God also love her? Perhaps God was angry with her because she did not keep herself sexually pure before marriage. Lot was not her first. First there was Ness, her best friend. Their secret affair went on for years, even though they both knew that they couldn't be with each other forever. Even though same sex relationships were commonplace, Jia's family would have never gone for it. She still couldn't remember who broke it off first, but the two agreed to remain friends. And friends they still were.

Then there was Rashad, who Jia was supposed to have married. Jia's father never liked Rashad because he was an artist. And scrawny.

"He will never amount to anything," Jia's father used to say. *"How is he going to support you and your children? Look at him! That is the look of someone who is starving. Do you want to starve, too?"*

Jia was unconcerned and knew that they would be just fine. The murals that covered their small one bedroom apartment told her that, together, they could accomplish anything. That was until Rashad was found dead, hanging by a rope in the apartment a week before their wedding. Though there was a suicide note left at the scene, Jia knew better. She didn't trust the situation, especially after her father married her off to Lot so quickly after Rashad's death.

"You need someone to take care of you," her father said. As if she, a grown-ass woman, couldn't take care of herself.

Maybe God was punishing her. Maybe God just didn't care about women. She had always heard God referred to as a man, maybe that was the source of her problem. Surely, if God was a woman, She would have seen Jia's plight and delivered her. Surely if God was a woman, She would have never tolerated the rape and abuse that Jia endured. Surely if God was a woman, other people would be able to see what she saw in Lot, and instead of envying her for having a "good man," would have held Lot accountable for his actions.

The visitors who were now at Jia's front door confirmed her theory. Jia awoke to their voices speaking to Lot, who was in the kitchen preparing breakfast for his guests. Lot didn't like to cook, but when he did, it was usually breakfast, consisting of eggs, sausage, and pancakes. Jia didn't eat meat, and years before going meatless she had refused to eat pork. It was just how she was raised. As Lot never adjusted his repertoire to accommodate Jia's dietary needs, she usually satisfied her hunger with pancakes and a bowl of fruit. This day would be no different.

Going into the kitchen, she kissed her husband on the cheek and greeted the visitors who were seated around the kitchen table. They called themselves messengers of God, two dark skinned men who went by Ronald and Devonte. They were both dressed in white, with bundles of lemongrass, sage, cedar, and lavender hanging from their necks like wreaths warding off a vampire, and AK-15s strapped to their backs— something that wasn't unusual because of the constant reality of violence.

Jia sat down next to Ronald with her bowl of fruit and a glass of water. She wasn't in the mood for pancakes. Her daughters, Constance and Patience, had already eaten and were in the other room watching reruns of Living Single on TV. More than a hundred and fifty years later, the cultural ethos that came out of the 1990s was still relevant!

Though the messengers had not said much, Jia could tell that there was something amiss. She just couldn't put her finger on it. The energy in the room felt heavy, like a weighted, wet blanket. And her spirit felt agitated. She could barely get through the bowl of fruit. And she felt this urge to fight, run, and cry all at the same time. Instead of initiating conversation, she waited for the messengers to either say something or for Lot to share what they had been talking about before she entered the room.

But Lot said nothing. He barely acknowledged Jia when she kissed him. He faced the pancakes that he was still flipping on the griddle, reaching the end of the batter. His silence added to the heaviness in the atmosphere that suffocated Jia.

"Good women don't misbehave. They don't talk back. They don't ask questions. They stay in their place."

Jia threw off the weight of her grandmother's words and opened her mouth to speak.

"Um . . ." she started. *"What is going on? Is something wrong?"*

Just as soon as the words had left her mouth, Lot reprimanded her.

"Silly woman," he said. *"Don't you know these are men of God. Don't embarrass me! Be quiet."*

"Good women listen and obey their husbands."

Ordinarily, a comment like that would have caused Jia to shrink back and shut up. That was the way her grandmother taught her. But something deep inside of her—whether it was the Holy Spirit, the ancestors, or her intuition—told her to keep speaking and gave her the strength to do so.

"*Lot please!*" Jia urged. She turned to Ronald and Devonte. "*Please tell us what is going on. I can tell something is wrong. No beating around the bush, either.*"

Devonte was the first to speak.

"Listen," he started. "*I don't know how to tell you all this, so I am going to just come out with it. We've been sent here by God to warn you and your family to leave Sodom. It's going to be destroyed in a matter of moments. The president has issued an executive order to kill and destroy all Black communities, and we don't have time to wait for the Supreme Court to overturn it. We have to act fast, now.*"

"*Ok,*" responded Jia while holding her chest and trying to breathe calmly. "*But where are we supposed to go? If the executive order is as serious as you say it is, nowhere is safe.*"

"*That's why we are here,*" said Ronald. "*We will take you and your family to an undisclosed location where you will be safe for the time being.*"

"*Why us, what did we do to earn this?*" Jia asked.

"*Because you have been identified as the only family who is righteous and God-fearing,*" said Devonte. "*God has heard the many prayers of your husband and is pleased with his devotion.*"

"*His devotion? His prayers?*" questioned Jia. "*Well, hasn't God heard my prayers? Hasn't God heard my cries? Doesn't God care enough about me to come and rescue me after all of these years?*"

"*Jia,*" screamed Lot. "*We have no time for that nonsense of yours. Shut up, get the kids, and let's get out of here. I've been telling you for years that this place will burn. I will not stick around for it, listening to your carrying on.*"

Jia was now in full-blown tears. After all this time, it was apparent to her that God didn't care about her or her experience. Her grandmother was wrong, because it didn't matter how much she obeyed her husband, didn't matter how well she kept house or raised her daughters, didn't matter that she prayed early in the morning before everyone else was up, didn't matter that she stayed in her place and kept quiet. Most of the time. Regardless of how hard she tried, she remained stuck. In that moment, Jia realized that she had the ability to do something different, even if it cost her.

"Give me an hour," Jia said.

"An hour?" questioned Ronald and Devonte in harmony.

"Yes, an hour. I will gather the kids' things and be ready to go. You all sit down and relax 'til then."

"One hour, Jia," Lot said. *"Not a minute more."*

Completely disregarding Lot, she looked toward the messengers who nodded in the affirmative.

She quickly threw the few belongings she had in a bag and packed her two teenage daughter's belongings as well. As she did, she pondered the messenger's words.

"Leave?"

Jia had spent all her adult life trying to make things better for her family and community. How many babies and children had she looked after as their parents went out to forage for food and bring home whatever resources they could put their hands on? How many times had she used the limited knowledge she had to nurture the sick and dying? How many committee meetings had she attended for the purpose of making their very claustrophobic and chaotic community better? She had labored, toiled, given everything she had inside of herself and more for the sake of this community that she had spent her entire life in. The roots went deep, and she couldn't abandon her community, not now, not ever, even as death and destruction loomed over their beautiful Black heads. But if she was going to leave, she was going to take as many people as she could with her, whether if Lot was pleased or not.

The packing took less than fifteen minutes. It gave her the remaining forty-five minutes to do what she did best: organize. Throwing on a worn pair of Timberland boots, Jia went door to door to warn her neighbors as the two messengers had warned her family. It was the least she could do.

She started with Fred and Ness right next door. They had twin sons who were a few years older than her girls. The two families had always joked that they would marry their children off to each other. Though a joke, Jia secretly hoped that it would come true and was delighted when her youngest daughter started dating Cory, one of their sons. Of all the families in their tight-knit community, she hoped that she could convince them to come with hers.

Jia didn't knock. She never did. She opened the back door and saw Ness standing in the kitchen, hovered over something she was making, as she always was. Ness was burning incense, Frankincense and Myrrh, Jia detected, and her hair was wrapped in a big white scarf, pulled back tightly into a low bun. And she smelled like coconut oil, just as she always did. Jia thought she looked beautiful against the sunlight that peeked through the window. There was no way she could leave her. Not now. Not ever.

"Girlfriend pack your things and get your kids. We've got to get the hell up out of here," Jia blurted out, realizing at that very moment how crazy she must sound.

"What the hell you talking about, J?" J was Ness' nickname for Jia. She always shortened people's names, even when it was only three letters long like Jia's.

"Like I said, sis, we got to go," she said, trying to breathe in between her fast-paced words. *"These men, they came to our door. They told us that danger is imminent, that the government is coming after all of us. We always thought they would completely do Black people in, and that day has come. We've got to get the hell up out of here. Now."*

Jia hated what was coming out of her mouth. She never wanted to be seen as an alarmist or a conspiracy theorist. There were plenty of those who had circulated in their small community over the years. Jia had always laughed at those people. Now she was one of those people.

"Fred," Ness screamed. *"Round up the guys and go on over to Lot's house."*

Fred, being in the very next room, acted fast, though he knew not what for. He often responded like this when it came to Ness. He doted on her and attended to her in ways that Lot never did with Jia. Ever since they had started dating, it had always been about Ness. Fred had no reason not to trust her, which made him mostly ignore the rumors that circulated about the closeness of Jia and Ness' relationship. People often hinted that there was something more there between the two women, but he refused to see, mostly because he could not imagine living without Ness in his life.

Fred grabbed an enormous bullhorn and started yelling loudly before he even left the house. Within seconds, people filled the streets and looked around to figure out what was happening. When they saw Fred walking towards Lot and Jia's house, they followed.

Lot came out of his house as he saw the crowd approaching. When he agreed to give Jia an hour, he didn't know what to make of it and definitely didn't know what to make of the crowd forming before him.

"*Lot,*" cried Fred. "*What's this I hear about these two messengers in your house stirring up trouble?*"

"*No trouble,*" said Lot. "*We've just been advised to quickly leave because danger is imminent. The government is coming around destroying all our communities. We need to get out of here before we are bombed and burned alive.*"

"*That sounds like trouble to me,*" replied Fred. "*Who are these people?*"

"*They are messengers of God.*"

"*How do you know? They could be the enemy sending us into an ambush.*" Fred wasn't being completely paranoid because he had heard of the same thing happening before. One simply couldn't be too trusting of others, even when they were well-intentioned. And to Fred, Lot wasn't too well-intentioned. He saw right through the facade Lot projected and didn't buy it.

"*Bring these messengers out so we can hear from them ourselves,*" someone screamed from the crowd that was still surrounding Lot's house. Others chimed in, adding their voice in agreement. The messengers appeared just as they were getting worked up. They wasted no time and without formal pleasantries reiterated the same things they had told Lot and Jia earlier.

"*Look, if we act fast, we can get to somewhere safe and protect ourselves along the way,*" one messenger started. "*All of us together can push off any would-be assailant if we are smart and fast. But we've got to act now.*"

"*Who are you, that we should believe you?*" asked Fred.

"We are messengers of God, sent to warn you all about what is about to happen," the other messenger said.

"Why should we trust you? How do we know you are not just trying to lead us straight into the arms of the enemy? Or that you are not trying to take over our community?" one of the other men from the crowd asked.

"You just have to trust us, and trust God."

"God?" asked Fred. *"Listen, we've heard that one before. Look, our families have been here trying to live off the grid for almost three generations. Ever since the Great Incident, we've been trying to protect ourselves from the government and preserve what little we have left of our culture, without that being swallowed up.*

"We've been here, working and toiling just trying to get by. Our men have patrolled our communities during the night to make sure we were safe, our women have kept us fed, and our children have kept joy in our hearts, giving us a reason to go on living day after day. We did this. Nobody came to help us, not the government, not no charity, and not no God.

"My grandfather, rest his soul, used to talk about this God. Used to say that our people trusted and believed in this God ever since the white man brought us over here and enslaved us. Made us abandon all our own cultural ways and relating to our own gods so we cannot even find them if we wanted to. Over five hundred and fifty years of shame, degradation, and brutalization that only increased after the Great Incident. Trust God? Nah man, I can't trust the white man's religion and if our people had only realized that from the beginning, maybe we wouldn't be in this mess. I would prefer to call on Obatala or whoever else could come and get us out of this hellhole, but I don't even know how to access them, how to pray to them, and I am so far removed from my sense of self that they don't even know who I am."

The crowd gathered around Fred nodded in agreement. Ness reached for his hand. Silence suffocated them all for what seemed like an eternity. It was clear that even after all these years of attending Bible studies and prayer meetings, that the people really didn't trust Lot. They trusted Fred. That's why they were standing behind Fred in this moment instead of behind Lot.

"Why would we lead you wrong? We've been your neighbors, your family for years. Why would we lie to you or deceive you? Trust us, come with us, let's get out of here and try to get our families somewhere safer."

"I don't trust you, Lot," said Fred. *"I know exactly who you are and have seen right through everything you have done. You didn't think God or anyone else was watching, did you? I was watching. I saw you. I saw the scars on Jia's body. I saw the tears on her face every single time she ran to our house for safety after fleeing yours. And so, no, I cannot trust you. And because I don't trust you, I don't trust these messengers of yours either."*

Turning toward the crowd that gathered behind him with baseball bats, Fred gave a final instruction. *"Let's get them all. Only leave Jia and the kids."*

The men surrounding Lot and Jia's house started to run with rapid intensity towards Lot and the messengers. Lot, though getting up there in years, was still quite strong. Without a moment's thought, he pushed Ron and Devonte out of the way, and put Jia and his daughters, Constance and Patience, in the direct path of the men who were now just beginning to bring their bats and other weapons down on the women who they initially wanted to protect. In their fury, they did not recognize that all their hostility was now being taken out on Jia and her children. It wasn't until Fred caught what was happening and yelled "stop," that the violence stopped. One by one, each backed away from the house.

In the frenzy of it all, Lot had gotten away. He didn't know where he was going, only that he was going. It was the messengers who stuck around and carried Jia and her daughters to safety. With Lot being only minutes ahead, they caught up to him quickly.

"Why in the hell did you do that?" screamed Jia. *"Why did you push us in front of those men? Why did you leave us? What the hell is going through your head right now?"*

"Listen, Jia," said Lot. *"You have a choice to make. You are going to be with me, or you are not. All this boo-hooing to your little friends about what goes on in our bedroom is out of line. You've embarrassed me to my core. I am so angry, I could take you out right now with my own hands."*

Under a moment of duress, all of Lot's pretense was finally falling away. Jia only hoped that the messengers were taking note. She hoped that God was paying attention. She knew that Lot had the capacity to harm her, but he had never been that way with the children. So, she decided to take a risk.

"Good women listen and obey their husbands."

"Ok, Lot!" she stated emphatically. *"I don't want to be with you. I have not wanted to be with you. Ever. There you have it. I don't know what that means for me, but I am not going with you anywhere."* Jia started to pull away, but her daughters clung fervently to her arms.

"Don't leave us," screamed Constance.

"Take us with you!" demanded Patience.

"Have it your way," said Lot. With all his strength, he ripped his daughters off their mother's arms and pulled them away. *"Stay here with these heathens you have grown to love so much, more than your own family, and perish."*

And perish she did. No sooner had she separated from her family, the gunfire and fire that now surrounded Sodom consumed her. But Jia did not cry. She did not even let out a whimper. Because even as the flames engulfed her thin frame, she knew she was finally free.

(3)

Lot came to laying in an empty warehouse next to his daughters, with little recollection about how he got there.

Not knowing where he was, he jumped up, half startled and half disoriented. Where was he? Where was his wife? Where were the messengers? What had happened? He felt drunk, but he knew that wasn't possible because he hadn't drunk in years. As his eyes adjusted to the darkness that surrounded him, he remembered all that had transpired, and it filled his heart with grief. He wished he were dead. After all they had been through, he wished he was with Jia. He wished he was anywhere but here.

He was beginning to feel the pangs of remorse over the way that he had treated her since the beginning of their marriage. He knew that he was shady from the very beginning. He was the one who, unsuspected by both Jia and her father, had snuck into their apartment the night Rashad died. He had first strangled Rashad so he passed out, then he hung him, so it appeared to be an act of suicide. He had longed for Jia since the days she was a young girl running around their neighborhood. He sometimes visited the small store where she worked beside Ness after school, just to get a glimpse of her sweet face. He never lingered; he didn't want his actions to be obvious. But he loved her. That's what he told himself the night he snuck in her apartment while Jia was away at work. And it was what he told himself when he came to Jia's father, right after Rashad's death, to persuade him to let him marry his daughter. And it was what he told himself every time they were together.

The only problem was, Jia never loved him, and he knew it. And he despised her for it. That's why he was so brutal, because she never yielded to him even though she did obey. Jia was good at minding her place, that wasn't Lot's issue. But she was never affectionate, she never got used to him, not after the birth of their children, not after more than twenty years of marriage.

And now she was gone. Really gone. Lot never imagined that she would ever actually leave him. He thought she was too scared to do so. No, he didn't want Jia to live in fear of him, but he was okay with it if it kept her doing what he wanted. But she did leave, taking the life that they had together with her.

Now all Lot had was his daughters, cuddled up in each other's arms just as they had done since they were babies. They were his only sense of comfort in this moment. He had to keep it moving for their sake, even if he did not know how or where.

Although he had the best of intentions, it took Lot a while to get things going after losing Jia. The somewhat aloof but hardworking Lot turned into someone completely unrecognizable. Most days he wasted away sleeping as his daughters forged for whatever food they could find. He did not have a clear sense of where they were, nor did he have great interest in trying to find out or finding another place.

Then there was this whole issue of starting another community. Was he really going to build another Sodom from the ground up? What gave him the reassurance that another community wouldn't also be destroyed? He did not want to put in all the blood, sweat, and tears for it to amount to absolutely nothing just as Sodom had.

And what about his daughters? They were young women now. They were getting to the point where they should soon be starting families of their own. But now that Sodom was destroyed and they were isolated from the rest of humanity, Lot did not see how that would be possible. Of course, there were more important things to worry about, but he couldn't help wondering how he was going to ensure the longevity of his family into the next generation. If his children didn't have children, who would carry on their family's legacy, who would tell their stories, who would make sure their names made it down in the history books—even if the books were oral accounts rather than written? He felt like he had an obligation to fight for and preserve what he could, even if it meant doing the unthinkable.

And the unthinkable he did. How do I know? Because I am a product of it. I am Jia, named after my great-grandmother. I am the daughter of Imani, the daughter of Constance, Lot and Jia's eldest daughter. Lot, as you may have guessed it, is my grandfather and great-grandfather. Lot raped both of his daughters, Constance and Patience, impregnating them both twice before killing himself for the shame that he had brought upon himself and his family.

Grandma Constance had three children, twin boys and a girl. And Great-Aunt Patience had two children, one boy and one girl. Together, Grandma Constance and Great-Aunt Patience found a place for our family to live, adjacent to a Black community that already existed. Our communities intermarried and continued to produce children. That's how I got here, some fifty-odd years after losing Great-Grandma Jia, more than a hundred and fifty years after the Great Incident.

No matter the span of time, it has not gotten any better for Black people in the United States. In fact, it has gotten worse. We barely have the capacity to breathe, let alone live and try to eke out some kind of existence. Our communities are always at risk of destruction and death. There is absolutely nothing left for us here so we have been rapidly leaving ever since we found out that if we can get to Mexico safely, we can get passports and a visa to go back to the continent. It feels awfully benevolent for Mexico to do such a thing, but the truth is they only want to shame the US—they really don't want us there either. Hence the visas. But at this point, we don't have the capacity to care whether we are being used for someone else's political gain—after all, that is the story of Black folks in this god-forsaken country from the beginning. We just want out; we will figure out all the details and implications as we go.

As we leave, we remember Lot's wife, Great-Grandma Jia, our beloved ancestor. Her story does not bring our family shame; it gives us great pride because she ultimately followed her heart and listened to her body. That's what makes her story worth remembering, worth recounting, worth telling our children for generations to come, because she threw off the yoke of oppression that women like her have carried since patriarchy was ever created. This is what makes her powerful! Because of her, all the people born in our family know how to stand against oppression, even when it is coming from within. We don't do family secrets around here, as we know secret shame has a way of killing us slowly. That's why Great-Grandma Jia felt so pushed against the wall. In order to heal our family's legacy, we must speak the truth. And speak it often.

And we also know how to construct new narratives and ways of being when the script we have been given is confining. Great-Grandma Jia was given a script by her own grandmother, a script about how good women should act. In pushing back against that script, she did not pass it down to us. She passed down strength instead, and we carry with us that strength, that vision she left for us—a vision that prioritized freedom above all else, even when that freedom could cost us our lives.

References

Anzaldúa, G. (1987). *Borderlands/La Frontera: The new mestiza.* San Francisco, CA: Aunt Lute Books.

Bell, D. (2004). The unintended lessons in brown v. board of education. *New York Law School Law Review, 49*(4), 1053-1068.https://heinonline.org/HOL/P?h=hein.journals/nyls49&i=1065&a=dW1uLmVkdQ

brown, a.m. (2017). *Emergent strategy: Shaping change, changing worlds.* AK Press: Chico, CA

Cone, J. (1997). God of the Oppressed. Maryknoll, NY: Orbis Books

Dillard, C.B. (2012). *Learning to (re)member the things we've learned to forget.* New York NY: Peter Lang Publishing.

Dillard, C.B. (2016). Turning the ships around: A case study of (re)membering as transnational endarkened feminist inquiry and praxis for Black teachers. *American Educational Studies Association, 52*(5), 406-423. Doi: 10.1080/00131946.2016.1214916.

Gladwell, M. (Producer). (2019). *Ms. Buchanan's Period of Adjustment.* [Audio Podcast]. Retrieved from http://revisionisthistory.com/episodes/13-miss-buchanans-period-of-adjustment?fbclid=IwAR1HrHlRbo8YqKmDGQbvKfBPoCbd1UVBMxCMybUQ3eAb0F0Vu_kSXmgLrEY

hooks, b. (1989). *Talking back: Thinking feminist, thinking Black.* Boston, MA: South End Press

hooks, b. (1994) *Teaching to transgress: Education as the practice of freedom.* New York: Routledge.

Lorde, A. (1984, 2007). *Sister outsider: Essays and speeches.* Toronto, ON: Crossing Press

McInnis, T. (2020, August 20). A farewell letter to DEI work. Inside Higher Ed. Retrieved August 22, 2020 from https://www.insidehighered.com/views/2020/08/20/diversi ty-equity-and-inclusion-offices-cant-be-effective-if-they-arent- empowered?fbclid=IwAR0TtoD- 4spjDbRETSmbrvW7CQyttjnnp- DIKIjCAW411_PQY8_fmvMzmo4

Neier, A. (2014, May 14). Brown vs. Board of Education: Key Cold War weapon. Reuters. Retrieved October 26, 2020 from https://www.reuters.com/article/idUS408043084620140514

Shange, N. (1989). *For colored girls who have considered suicide/when the rainbow is enuf: A choreopoem.* Ann Arbor, MI: University of Michigan

Tinsley, O.N. (2008). Black Atlantic, Queer Atlantic: Queer imaginings of the Middle Passage. *GLQ ,14* (2-3): 191–215. doi:10.1215/10642684-2007-030

Underwood, M. (2016). "Battered love": Exposing abuse in the book of Job. In Bryon, G.L & Lovelace, V. (eds.) *Womanist interpretations of the Bible: Expanding the discourse, p. 165 - 184.* Atlanta, GA: SBL Press.

Walker-Barnes, C. (2014*). Too heavy a yoke: Black women and the burden of strength.* Eugene, OR: Cascade Books

Weems, R. (1993). *I asked for intimacy: Stories of blessings, betrayals, and birthings.* San Diego, CA: LuraMedia

Woods, J. (2016). Holy [Recorded by Jamila Woods]. On *Heavn* [CD]. Chicago, IL: Jagjaguwar

Wood, J. (2019). Basquait [Recorded by Jamila Woods & Saba]. On *Legacy! Legacy!* [CD]. Chicago, IL: Jagjaguwar

Williams, D. (1993). A womanist perspective on sin. In E. Townes (Ed). T*roubling in my soul: Womanist perspectives on evil and suffering (*pp. 130 - 149). Maryknoll, NY: Orbis Books

To find out more about Ebony Adedayo visit
https://ebonyjohanna.com/

or

IG: ebonyadedayo

Other books by Ebony Adedayo:

Embracing a Holistic Faith: Essays on Biblical Justice
(Released April 2014)

Incomplete Stories: On Loss, Love, and Hope
(To be released July 2021)